◆ Then check the back-of-the-book section, "To th[e]
Book" (pp. 190-197), for an outline of social underst[andings,]
behavior traits, and map understandings developed throughout *In the Neighborhood*.

The material printed in blue will help you picture yourself teaching from this book

◆ These brief teaching suggestions are exactly as they will appear on the pupils'
pages of the Teacher's Edition. Along with guide questions to ask of the class,
you'll find brief summaries of the purpose of each selection and reminders of appro-
priate trips and special projects to tie in with a particular story lesson. (More
detailed suggestions are given in the complete lesson plans contained in the Guidebook section of the Teacher's Edition.)

The chart below offers a selection of story lessons to sample

◆ In the left-hand column are listed a few of the stories in this book about people
at work or at play, doing things with which children in *any* neighborhood can identify themselves. The chart also gives page references to the study pages which
follow each story and contain related pictures, questions, and information, and to
the pages in the back-of-the-book section that summarize the social understandings
and behavior traits highlighted in each story listed.

GOOD NEIGHBORS HELP EACH OTHER

STORY	RELATED STUDY PAGES	SOCIAL UNDERSTANDINGS DEVELOPED	BEHAVIOR TRAITS EMPHASIZED
Help for Mr. Long, pp. 26-30	31	191	194
The Newspaper Helps Judy, pp. 42-47	48, 49	192	194
At the Store, pp. 106-113	114, 115	193	195

GOOD NEIGHBORS HAVE FUN TOGETHER

STORY	RELATED STUDY PAGES	SOCIAL UNDERSTANDINGS DEVELOPED	BEHAVIOR TRAITS EMPHASIZED
Old and New Schools, pp. 32-37	38	191	194
Neighborhood Fun, pp. 72-77	78, 79	192	195
Christmas in the New Neighborhood, pp. 171-177	178, 179	194	195

THE BASIC SOCIAL STUDIES PROGRAM

CURRICULUM FOUNDATION SERIES
REG. U. S. PAT. OFF.

In the Neighborhood

Discuss meaning of *neighborhood*. Establish that a neighborhood is made up
of all the families of the children that go to one elementary school.

Explore children's knowledge of the area served by your school.

by Paul R. Hanna and Genevieve Anderson Hoyt

William S. Gray, *Reading Advisor*

Illustrated and Designed by Jack White

Scott, Foresman and Company
Chicago Atlanta Dallas Palo Alto Fair Lawn, N.J.

Note: Brief suggestions for guiding the reading and discussion
of each selection appear in blue type on each page.
New words are italicized.

See "Introducing *In the Neighborhood*" in the *Guidebook*.

To the Children Who Read This Book

Explain that this is a letter from the authors of this book.

The name of this book tells you that
it is a book about neighborhoods.

Guide the reading of each paragraph.

Look at the pictures on your book.

They are pictures of neighborhoods.

The book tells about the neighborhoods.

Find the picture in which you see
many big old houses.

"Does anyone in our neighborhood *live* in an *apartment building?*"

What other buildings are
in the picture?

Find the picture in which you see
farm buildings.

Find the picture of a new neighborhood.

What tells you that this is
a new neighborhood?

Find the picture in which you see
apartment buildings.

Is there a school in every picture?

2

Reading this book will help you learn
new things about your neighborhood.

Talking about what you read
will help you learn, too.

No book can tell you all
that you want to know.

You will want to look at everything
in your neighborhood.

You will want to talk about what you see.

You will want to talk to your neighbors.

You will want to find out what they do.

In what other ways can you learn
about your neighborhood?

Which picture makes you think
of where you live?

Find a picture like it in your book.

Read to find out all about the neighborhood
that makes you think of yours.

Then read about the other neighborhoods.

Note: Each section is like a little book. Sections can be read in any order.
See Page 198 for vocabulary statement.
See "How to Use In the *Neighborhood*" in the "Golden Section."

These pages illustrate the home of the main character in each section.

David Hall's Neighborhood

Judy Taylor's Neighborhood

Mike Longway's Neighborhood

4

Linda West's Neighborhood

Steve Bell's New Neighborhood

Your Own Neighborhood

David Hall's Neighborhood

David Hall lives in the country.
His home is on a farm.

If children have read *At School*, they will be familiar with David Hall.

Identify members of the Hall family.
"Father and the boys are going out
to do *their* work in the *field*."

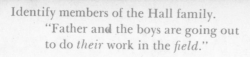

Lost in the Country

"Come, boys," said Mr. Hall.

"It is time to go to the field.
We have work to do."

"Me, too?" asked David.

"You, too!" said his big brother, Jim.
"There is work for all of us on this farm."

"I can work, too," said Kathy.

"Yes, you can," said her mother.
"You are a big help in the house, Kathy.

I would not know what to do
without you."

The boys went to the field with their father.
Kathy helped her mother do the housework.

"What can I do now?" asked Kathy.

"You may hide," said Mrs. Hall.

"I will put Jack to sleep, and
then I will find you."

So Mother went to put Jack to sleep.

And Kathy ran away to hide.

When Mrs. Hall came back,
she looked for Kathy.

She looked in every room, but Kathy
was not in the house.

"Where do you suppose Kathy went to hide?"

"Where is Mother looking?"
"Do you suppose Mother *rang* the bell?"

Then Mrs. Hall went out and looked
in the barn. But Kathy was not in the barn.

Mrs. Hall looked everywhere, but
she could not find Kathy.

She called and called. But Kathy
did not come.

So she rang the bell to call
Father and the boys.

They came to see what Mother wanted.

Discuss where Mother looked for
Kathy and why she rang the bell.

"Kathy is lost!" said Mrs. Hall. "Let's see how many neighbors mother called on the *telephone*."

"I have looked everywhere for her."

"Telephone the neighbors," said Mr. Hall.
"They will help us find her."

So Mother went in and called the neighbors.

Mrs. Day said, "Kathy lost! Oh, dear!
We will come and help you look for her."

"We will get our car and come,"
said Mrs. Peters.

"We will come right away," said Mrs. Long.

All the other neighbors said that they
would come and look for Kathy, too.

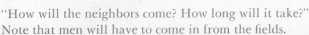
"How will the neighbors come? How long will it take?"
Note that men will have to come in from the fields.

"Where do you think the neighbors looked for Kathy?"
"Do you think she may have gone to the road?"

Soon all the neighbors were there.

Some of them went with Mrs. Hall
to look in the house again.

Some went with Mr. Hall to look
in the barn again.

Mr. Peters went in his car to look up
and down the roads.

Mr. Long and his two boys went
with David to look in the field.

In the field there was corn everywhere.

It was a very big cornfield.

Mr. Long and the three boys went
up the field.

They went down the field.

They called and looked for Kathy.

"Where do you suppose Kathy is?"
"Who do you think will find her?"

"Were you *right?*"

At last David found Kathy.

"Here she is!" he called to the others.

"She went to sleep."

Kathy looked up in surprise.

"Where is Mother?" she asked.

"Mother let me hide. She is looking for me."

"Everyone is looking for you!"
laughed Mr. Long.

Then they went back to the house.

David rang the bell again. This time it was
to tell everyone that Kathy was found.

"Why was it hard to find Kathy?"

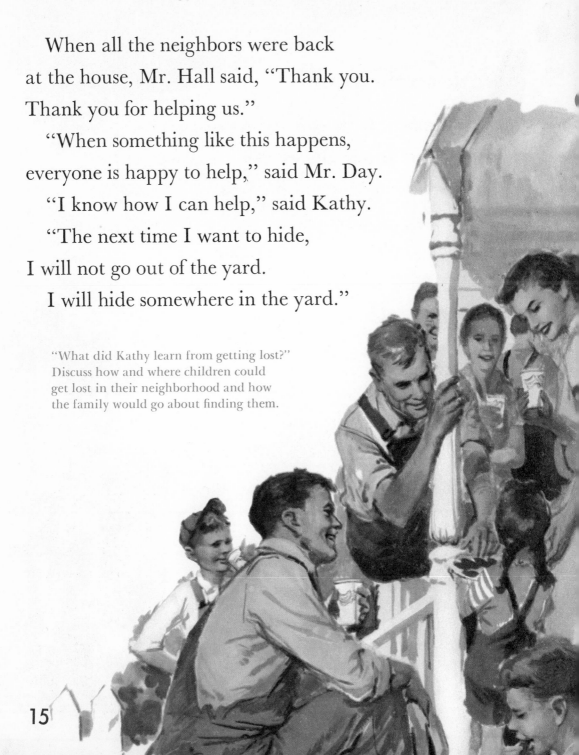

When all the neighbors were back
at the house, Mr. Hall said, "Thank you.
Thank you for helping us."

"When something like this happens,
everyone is happy to help," said Mr. Day.

"I know how I can help," said Kathy.

"The next time I want to hide,
I will not go out of the yard.

I will hide somewhere in the yard."

"What did Kathy learn from getting lost?"
Discuss how and where children could
get lost in their neighborhood and how
the family would go about finding them.

"Have any of you ever worked in a *garden?*"
"What have you helped *pick?*"
"How do you help with the work at home?"

Work on the Farm

On the Hall farm there is work to do
in the house and in the garden.

There is work to do in the fields.

There are things to pick.

There are animals to take care of.

What work are the Halls
doing in the pictures?

What work does your family do?

Compare and contrast work done by the
Halls with work in your neighborhood.

The Halls use machines to help them
with some of their work.

Look at the pictures.

How do the machines help the Halls?

How do machines help with the work
in your home?

Discuss how machines help with the work
of families in your neighborhood.

Mr. Hall uses big machines to help
with his work in the field.

Here you see some of the machines
he uses to raise and pick his corn.

What is he doing in each picture?

What machines does your father
use to help with his work?

Discuss sequence of plowing, planting, harrowing, cultivating, and harvesting.
     Identify each machine and the tractor.
Discuss machines children have seen used to produce food in your neighborhood.

18

Open Gates

"I wonder how many *gates* were left open and who forgot to close them."

"Let's see if we can find out on this page."

"David! David!" called Mr. Hall.

"Jim and I are going up the road to see Mr. Long.

Do you want to go with us?"

"Yes, I do," David called back.

He opened the garden gate and ran to Kathy.

"Here, Kathy," he said. "Take this to Mother."

Then away went David with his father and Jim.

"Do you think David closed the garden gate?"
Identify the Long's farm "Up the road." (see page 39)

19

"Whose calves do you think they are?"

When they came to the Bell farm,
David said, "Look, Jim.

See all the calves in Mr. Bell's lot."

"They are beautiful calves," said Jim.
"Mr. Bell must take good care of them."

The Halls did not see that the gate
to the lot was open just a little.

But soon one of the calves did, and
out of the lot he ran.

Out ran the other calves, too.

Down the road they all went.

"Whose calves were they?" Locate Bell farm on pages 6-7.
"Did the calves go in the same direction that the Halls are going?"
"Read the sentence that tells you. Where do you think they went first?"

20

"Where are the calves *by*
the time the *mailman* sees them?"
"Where do you suppose the calves will go next?"

The mailman saw the calves run
into the churchyard.

"I must go and tell Mr. Bell about his calves,"
said the mailman.

So he went on up the road to tell Mr. Bell
about his calves right away.

By that time the calves ran out of the churchyard.

Down the road they went to the Day farm.

Mrs. Day saw them and said, "Oh, dear.
I must call the Bells and tell them
their calves are here."

 "Where do you think the mailman will find Mr. Bell?"

The mailman saw Mr. Bell in a field.

"Your calves are out!" called the mailman.

"I saw them down at the church."

"Thanks for telling me," Mr. Bell called,
and he ran to get his pick-up truck.

Then the mailman went on up the road.

Soon he met Mr. Hall and the two boys
on their way home.

"Mr. Bell's calves are out,"
called the mailman.

"We will look for them,"
Mr. Hall called back.

"What kind of *truck* did the Halls have?"

"Who is going in the same direction as the calves now?"
"Do you think that the Halls will find the calves?"
"Where?"

22

After talking to the mailman, the Halls went on down the road. On the way they looked for Mr. Bell's calves.

And guess where they found them?

Right in the Hall garden!

Mrs. Hall and Kathy were in the garden, too.

"Get out! Get out!" they were calling.

Just then Mr. Bell came.

The calves ran this way and that way, and the Halls and Mr. Bell ran after them.

But at last they got all the calves out of the garden.

They put the calves in the barn lot.

"Who *got* the calves into this lot?"

23

Then everyone came back to look
at the garden.

Mr. Hall asked, "How did this happen?
How did the calves get into our garden?"

"I must have left the gate to my lot open,"
said Mr. Bell.

"And I guess I left our garden gate open,"
said David.

Mr. Bell looked at David and said,
"Just look at your mother's garden!
It is up to us to do something about it."

"What can we do?" asked David.

Mr. Bell said, "I know what we can do.
You help me take my calves home now.
We will get something from my garden
for your mother.

Then after this you can come to my garden
to get what your mother wants."

"Oh, thank you!" said David. "And I can
tell you one thing, Mr. Bell. I will see to it
that your garden gate is not left open!"

"Could something like this happen in our neighborhood?"
"What do you think of Mr. Bell's idea?"
Help children retrace the route the calves took. Use pages 6-7 as guide.

24

Rules in a Country Neighborhood

A good farm neighbor takes care
of his gates and his animals.

He does not let his animals run out
into the road.

He does not let his animals get
into another neighbor's fields.

He does not let his dog run
after farm animals, cars, and people.

When one farm neighbor uses another's
machine, he takes good care of it.

He takes it back right away.

People must walk on the left
on a country road.

Which rules are good ones
for your neighborhood?

Discuss reasons for having neighborhood rules.
Compare and contrast rules suggested with those in your neighborhood.
"Why do different neighborhoods have different rules?"

"Someone gets *hurt* in this story.
He was on a corn *picker*."

Help for Mr. Long

The children in the country neighborhood
all went to the little country school.

Mrs. Long was their teacher.

One day Mrs. Bell ran into the schoolhouse.

"Oh, Mrs. Long," she said. "Mr. Long
is hurt. He was on the corn picker
out in the field."

"I had a feeling something like this
would happen," said Mrs. Long.

"Our corn picker is an old machine."

"You go right home," said Mrs. Bell.
"I will take care of the children."

So Mrs. Long went home, and Mrs. Bell
helped the children with their schoolwork.

"Where have you seen a picture of a corn picker?" (page 18)
If children read *At School* last year recall visit of Susan's class to this school.

The next day Mr. and Mrs. Long looked
down the road.

"Here come our neighbors!" said Mrs. Long
in surprise.

The neighbors came into the yard.

"Hello, hello," they all called. "We have
come to help you out."

The neighbor women went into the house.

And the men went into the cornfield.

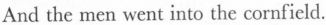

"How can you tell that some of the men brought tractors?"
"Find the corn *crib* on the page."

Up and down the field went
the big corn pickers.

Into the trucks went the corn.

Some of the men took the trucks
to the cribs.

Other men put the corn
into the cribs.

Then back to the field
went the men with the trucks.

"What do you think the men do next?"

The men came in from the cornfield at noon.
The women had a big dinner for them.

In the afternoon the men went back to the field.

When all the corn was picked and in the cribs,
some of the neighbors went home.

But some men went to the barnyard.

They helped Mr. Long's boys take care of
the farm animals.

Then they all went home to do their work.

"What farm work are the men and boys doing?"

29

"What day do you think the children came to help?" (*Saturday*)

On Saturday the school
children came to the Long farm.

Into the cornfield they ran.

They picked up the corn that
the corn picker had missed.

Jim Hall took the corn to the cribs.

By noon all the corn was in the cribs.

Mrs. Long called the children in
to eat dinner.

"How did you think of helping like this?"
she asked them.

Judy Peters said, "Everyone wanted
to help you and Mr. Long. Mrs. Bell said
this would help."

"And it did help us," said Mrs. Long.

"You are very good corn pickers."

"How did the children's work help?"
"Why did some of the corn fall to the ground?"
"If you do not know, look at the picture of the cornpicker on page 28 again."

Many Things Are Raised

What will Mr. Long do
with the corn he raised?

What do you eat that is made from corn?

In which pictures do you see something
that is raised for food?

In which pictures do you see something
that is used to make clothes?

What is raised in your neighborhood?

31

"Which school do you think is old?"
"What do you suppose the new school will be like?"

Old and New Schools

"David's father and mother are Tom and Susan Hall's *uncle* and *aunt*. What relation is David to Tom and Susan?"
"How do you know that his father and their father are brothers?"

It was the last day of school.

All the neighbors were at school.

Other people were there, too.

David's Grandfather and Grandmother Hall
had come.

His Uncle Dick and Aunt Sally Hall were there.

And his cousins Tom and Susan and Peter.

Identify members of Hall family.

"Come here, everyone," said Uncle Dick.

"Look at these old pictures that someone put up."

The Halls went to look at the pictures on the schoolhouse.

"Just look at the first picture," said Grandfather Hall.

"It shows how the school looked when I was a boy.

That was a long time ago.

What good times I had here!"

33

"Now look at this picture, David,"
said his Uncle Dick.

"It shows how the school looked
when your father and I were boys."

"The school had a bell, then,"
said Tom's father.

"I rang that bell many times to call
the children in.

The school does not look the same
without the old bell."

"Now look at this," said Jim. "This is
a picture of our new school.

This is where we will go next fall."

"If you were David how would you feel about going to the new school?"

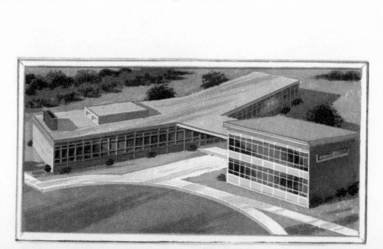

Everyone but David was happy
about the new school.

"I know that I have to go
to the new school," he said.

"But I like our old school.

The new one is so big that I will not
know many of the children."

"Oh, David," said Tom.

"You will make new friends.

You will like the new school
when you get there."

"But what will happen to our old school?"
David asked.

His father said, "It would make a
good farm building.

It would make a good building for our farm."

"Yes, it would," said Grandfather Hall.
"And I know what I will do. I will buy it
for your farm.

Then David can see his old school every day."

"How did David feel?"
"Let's see what happened to the old school."

Grandfather did buy
the old schoolhouse.

The neighbors helped take it
to the Hall farm.

Two of the men made a big door
in the old school.

The new door was so big that the
farm machines could go right in.

Then Mr. Hall and Jim painted
the building.

David looked at the old school.

"It was a good school," he said.

"And now it is a good farm building."

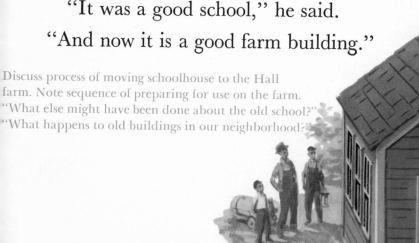

Discuss process of moving schoolhouse to the Hall
farm. Note sequence of preparing for use on the farm.
"What else might have been done about the old school?"
"What happens to old buildings in our neighborhood?"

"Why did David have to go to the new school in a *bus?*"

In the fall David went to the new school.

How surprised he was the first day!

A school bus came to take the Hall children
to the new school.

There were many children in the big bus.

David liked the ride to school.

"What do you suppose he liked *best* about the new school? Let's see."

He liked the new school, too.

There was a beautiful yard and a
big place to play.

When the children went in, the principal
met them. He showed them where to find
their rooms.

David liked his beautiful room.

He liked everything about the new school.

But best of all, Mrs. Long was his teacher again.

Discuss means of transportation used to get to school in
your neighborhood. See suggestions for guiding discussion
of ways of adjusting to change in *Guidebook* lesson plan.

"Some of the things you see in the pictures are used today.
Others were used many *years ago*."
"Read the page and do what the last two sentences tell you to do."

Old Ways and New Ways

Grandfather and Grandmother Hall lived on the Hall farm many years ago.

They did many of the same things that David's family does.

Look at these pictures. Find the old and the new way of doing the same thing.

Long Farm

Bell Farm

Peters Farm

Side Road

School

Church

Good Farm

Main Road

Gates Farm

Day Farm

Hall Farm

Side Road

"How is this picture map like the picture on pages 6-7?" "How is it different?" (labels)

This is a picture map of David's neighborhood.

How many farms are there in this neighborhood?

Find the Hall farm.

Which way did each family go
when they helped Mr. Long?

How did the calves go from the Bell farm
to the Hall farm?

What can you tell about David's neighborhood
by reading the picture map?

See "Making and Reading Maps" in "Golden Section."
Note particularly suggestions for teaching directions.

Compare and contrast with the children's own neighborhood.

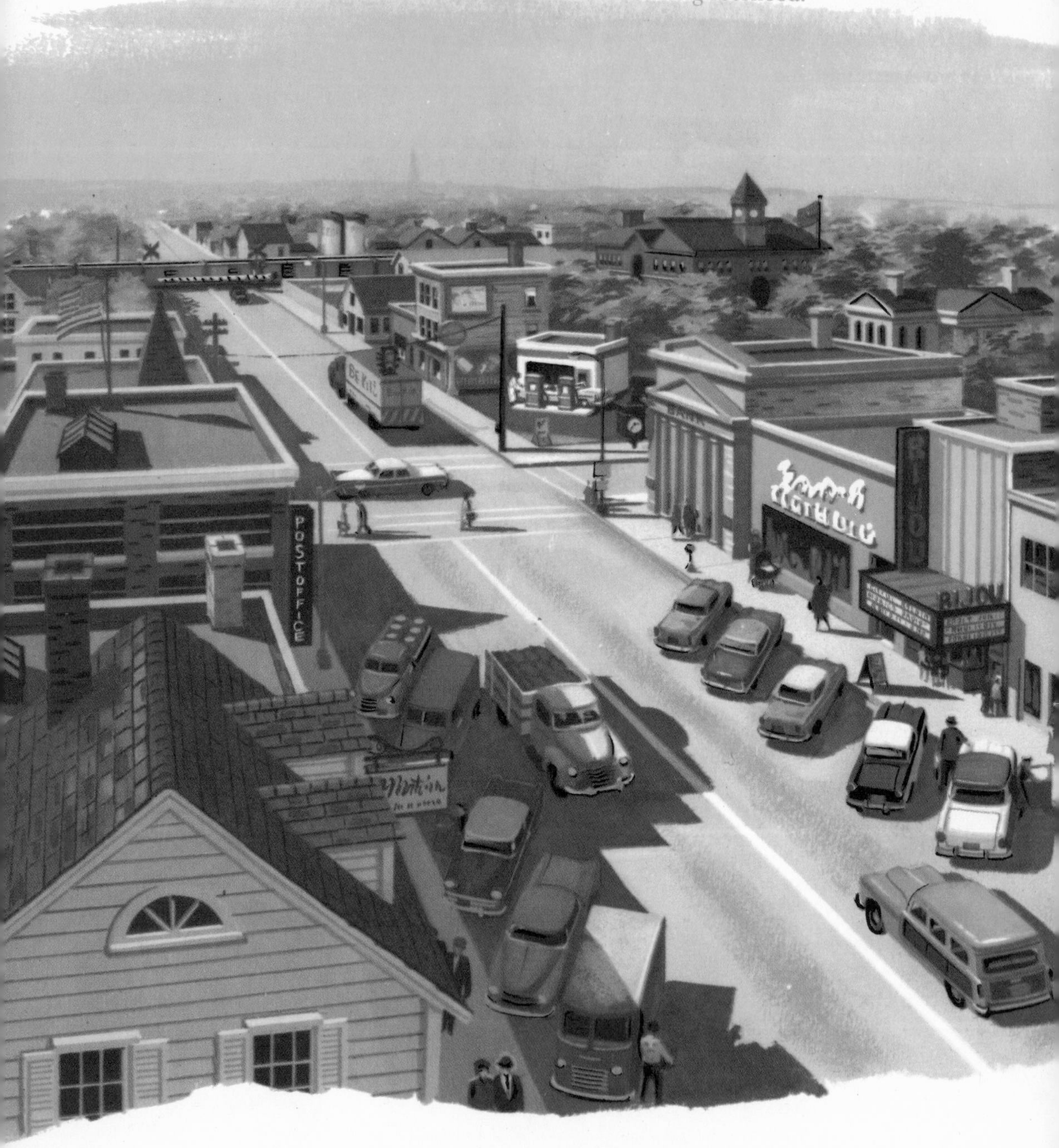

Judy Taylor's Neighborhood

Judy Taylor lives in this neighborhood.
She lives in a big white house.

The Newspaper Helps Judy

Judy Taylor was teaching her little bird to talk.

Judy said, "My name is Pretty Boy! My name is Pretty Boy!"

The bird looked at Judy.

"Pretty Boy! Pretty Boy!" it said.

But that was all Pretty Boy said.

Just then Judy's brother Jack ran into the house.

"Pretty Boy! Pretty Boy!" said the bird.

And out of the house it went.

"What do you think Judy is *teaching* Pretty Boy?"

Judy and Jack ran after the bird.

Judy called, "Oh, Pretty Boy. Where
are you? Please come back!"

The children called and called.

They looked and looked.

But they could not find Pretty Boy.

Some of the neighbors looked for
Judy's bird, too.

But no one could find it.

Pretty Boy was lost!

"What do you think Judy will
do to find her lost bird?"

The next morning Judy went
from room to room in her school.

She asked all the children
about Pretty Boy.

But no one had found her bird.

Then Dick Ball said, "Talk to my father.

He will write a story about Pretty Boy
and put it in his newspaper.

Everyone reads The Home News."

44

When school was out, Judy went
to see Dick's father.

She asked Mr. Ball to put a story
about Pretty Boy in his newspaper.

"It is a good thing you came now,"
said Mr. Ball.

"Our newspaper will go out in the morning.

But I will have time to write a story
about your lost bird now.

Everyone can read the story.

Then we will see what happens."

"How do you think the telephone helped Judy? Who answered the telephone when it rang?"

The next morning Mrs. Taylor's telephone rang.

When she said, "Hello!" someone said, "I am Mrs. White.

I live at 125 Church Street.

I see the story in The Home News about your lost bird.

A little bird that talks came to our house. I think it may be yours."

"Oh, thank you," said Mrs. Taylor. "When Judy gets home, we will come and see the bird."

Identify Mrs. Taylor and Mrs. White. "Why did Mrs. White call Mrs. Taylor?"

After school Judy and her mother went to Mrs. White's house.

When the bird saw Judy, it called, "Pretty Boy! My name is Pretty Boy!"

"Oh, Mother!" said Judy. "Did you hear?
He talked! Pretty Boy talked!"

"Yes, Judy," said Mrs. Taylor.

Then she said to Mrs. White, "Thank you
for calling us.

You can see how happy Judy is."

"The bird is happy, too," said Mrs. White.

"I did not know the bird was Judy's.

Then I saw the story in the morning newspaper
and called you."

"We are happy you did," said Mrs. Taylor.

"You must come to see us sometime."

"I would like to," said Mrs. White. "But
what would I do with the children?"

"If you will come, I will help take care of
the children," said Judy.

"Oh, thank you, Judy," said Mrs. White.
"I will come soon."

"Now, Judy, we must go," said Mrs. Taylor.

"Yes," said Judy, "for I must tell
Mr. Ball that we have found Pretty Boy!"

"What would Judy have done *if* there had been no newspaper to help her?"

How a Telephone Helps Us

How did the telephone help Judy find her bird?

Name some ways the telephone helps you or someone in your family.

What do you say when someone calls and asks for your mother?

What do you do if she is not at home?

What do you want to find when you look in a telephone book?

Who would you call if you saw a fire? What would you say?

Who would you call if you found someone that was lost? What would you say?

Who would you call if someone were hurt? What would you say?

Teach children how to use a telephone book.

What stores in your neighborhood would you call to get something to eat?

48

How a Newspaper Helps Us

"Could you read anything in the newspaper a year ago?"

This year you will want to look in the newspaper to find out many things.

What do you read in the newspaper every day?

What does the newspaper tell you about schools?

What church news can you find in the newspaper?

What does the newspaper tell about the stores in your neighborhood?

What other things does the newspaper tell you about your neighborhood?

What can you find in the newspaper about things that happened a long time ago?

Summarize how a telephone and a newspaper can be used by the children in your neighborhood.

Halloween Pictures

Jack and his friend Jim Little were
helping Mr. Taylor in his store.

"It is about time for Halloween,"
said Mr. Taylor.

"What are you boys going to do
to have fun this year?"

"How can we have fun in this neighborhood?"
asked Jim. "There is not a thing to do
here on Halloween."

"I know something we could do," said Jack.

"Where my cousin lives, the children make
pictures on store windows for Halloween."

"We could not do that here," said Jim.

"Our neighborhood may surprise you, Jim,"
said Mr. Taylor.

"What do you think
Mr. Taylor will do?"

The next morning Mr. Taylor went
from store to store on Main Street.

"Will you help the children have fun
on Halloween this year?" he asked.

"Could the boys and girls make
pictures on your windows?"

Everyone on Main Street wanted to help
with the Halloween fun.

Everyone but Mr. Read!

"No pictures on my window," he said.
"I want everyone to see into my store."

"It is up to you," said Mr. Taylor.
"Then the children will make pictures
on all the windows but yours."

Mr. Taylor talked to the principal and
the teachers at Jack's school.

Then the teachers talked to the children.

The children said that they would like
to make Halloween pictures.

"Where did the children paint pictures?"

Soon it was the day to paint the pictures.

Up one side of Main Street and down the other the children went to work.

Some painted pictures on store windows.

Some painted pictures on the windows of other buildings.

But no one painted a picture on Mr. Read's window.

The children in Judy's room painted pictures on Mr. Ball's window.

The pictures were so good that Mr. Ball put a story about them in his newspaper.

"How do you know that the pictures were very good?"

The next day was Saturday.

Everyone came to Main Street to see the Halloween pictures.

They walked from store to store looking at the pictures.

Some of the pictures were funny and made everyone laugh.

"How did Mr. Read feel when no one looked at his window on *Saturday?*"
"What do you think he will do?"

Everyone had a good time.

Everyone but Mr. Read.

There were no pictures on his window.

No one looked at his store.

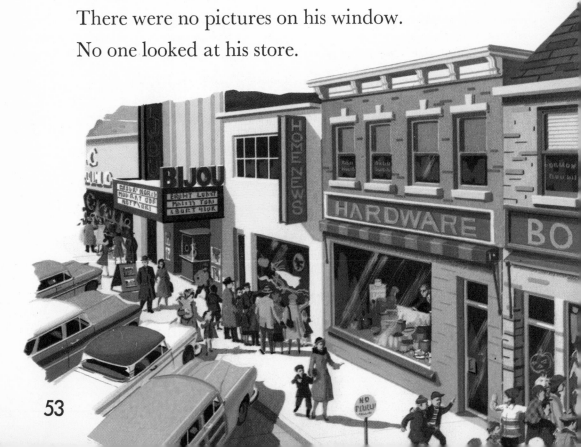

That night Mr. Read went to see Mr. Taylor.

He told Mr. Taylor that he wanted
pictures on his window after all.

Mr. Taylor said, "Ask the boys and girls
in Jack's room.

They would like to paint pictures for you."

"I will," said Mr. Read.

And that is just what Mr. Read did.

The children in Jack's room painted
funny pictures on Mr. Read's window.

Mr. Read laughed when he saw the pictures.

"Thank you, children. It was good of you
to come back and do this for me," he said.

On the way back to school, Jack asked Jim,
"What do you think about our neighborhood now?"

"I was surprised," said Jim.

"Everyone wanted us to have Halloween fun.

And they all helped when they found out
what we wanted to do."

Fun in Your Neighborhood

What do you do to have fun on Halloween?

Could you do what the children
in Judy's neighborhood did?

Name some other ways to have fun
in the fall of the year.

What do you do to have fun
other times of the year?

Which pictures show ways you can
have fun in your neighborhood?

Discuss activities shown and questions asked.

"What do you suppose Jack will learn about rules?"
"Do you think he learns about *bicycle* rules?"

Jack Learns about Rules

"What is Jack doing in the picture that he *should* not be doing?"

"I am going down to Jim's house,"
Jack called to Judy.

"What do you think will happen?"

Then away he went down the sidewalk
on his new bicycle.

"Jack!" called Judy. "Father said
you should ride in the street."

But Jack did not hear what Judy said.

So on he went down the sidewalk.

Karen Read was on her way home
from the store.

She was talking to Mrs. White.

She did not see Jack on his bicycle.

When Jack saw Karen, he did not know
how to stop.

"Look out!" he called.

Karen jumped, but Jack ran right into her.

Down went the bicycle and Jack.

Down went Karen and all the things
from the store.

This way and that way they all went.

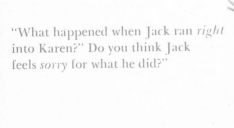

"What happened when Jack ran *right*
into Karen?" Do you think Jack
feels *sorry* for what he did?"

"What do you suppose Jack will do now?"

Mrs. White helped Karen get up.

"Are you hurt, Karen?" she asked.

"No," said Karen. "I am not hurt,
but just look at my things.

What will my mother say?"

"How about you, Jack?" asked Mrs. White.
"Are you hurt?"

"No, I am all right," said Jack.
Then he looked at Karen.

"I am sorry, Karen," he said.
"I will help you take your things home
and tell your mother what happened.

Will that be all right?"

"Oh, yes," said Karen. "That would be
a big help!"

Jack went home with Karen and told
Mrs. Read what had happened.

"I am sorry, Mrs. Read," he said.

"When I saw Karen, I did not know
how to stop my new bicycle."

"I am sorry, too," said Mrs. Read.
"But you should learn how to stop
your bicycle."

"I want to," said Jack. "And I know now
that I should learn to ride my bicycle
in the street."

Mrs. Read said, "Maybe our council can find
a way to teach you."

The next night the council had a meeting.
Mrs. Read went to the meeting.

She told the council what had happened
to Karen and Jack.

The people on the council said, "We should
have made some bicycle rules long ago.

Someone should teach children where and
how to ride their bicycles."

The next night Mr. Taylor was reading
his newspaper. "Here is something
you should know, Jack," he said.

"The council had a meeting last night,
and made some rules."

"What rules did they make?" asked Jack.

Mr. Taylor said, "One rule is that
children with big bicycles must ride
in the street.

Another rule is that two children must
not ride on one bicycle.

Everyone with a new bicycle can go
to the school next Saturday.

Mr. Ball will teach you the safe way
to ride in the street."

"I will be there," said Jack.

"I did not hurt Karen, but the next
time I could hurt someone."

"Yes," said his father. "And that someone
could be you."

Neighborhood Bicycle Rules

What rules are there about bicycles in your neighborhood?

Who made the rules?

What do the rules say about how to ride bicycles in the street?

Why is it not safe for two children to ride on a bicycle?

On which side of the street do you ride?

Why is it not safe to ride on the sidewalk?

What could happen if you forgot a rule?

WHICH IS THE RIGHT WAY? WHY?

61

Other Rules

Does a council make rules
for your neighborhood?

What rules made by the council help
keep the neighborhood beautiful?

What rules help keep you safe when
you go to school?

Develop understanding that neighborhood rules affect living in a neighborhood in many ways.

What rules help keep you safe when
you play?

Which children in the pictures
forgot a rule?

The Church Social

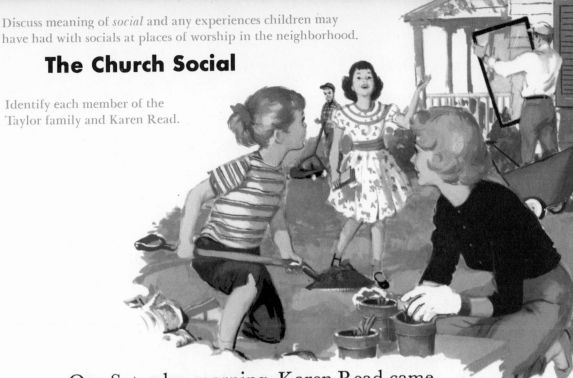

One Saturday morning, Karen Read came
to see Mrs. Taylor.

"Mrs. Taylor," she said, "our church wants
to buy playthings for our baby room.

So we are going to have a social
next Friday night. Will you come?"

"The Taylor family will be there,"
said Mrs. Taylor. "We like church socials."

"But what is a baby room?" asked Judy.

"You will see at the social on Friday,"
said Karen. And away she ran.

"Why did Karen come to see the Taylors?"

Everyone in Karen's church was busy.

The boys and girls were busy.

They went from house to house
to tell about the social.

They went up and down Main Street, too.

All the mothers were busy.

They made cakes and cookies.

On the day of the social
the fathers were busy, too.

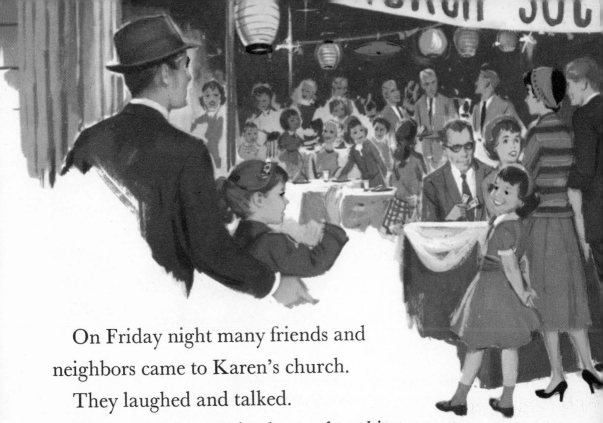

On Friday night many friends and
neighbors came to Karen's church.

They laughed and talked.

They liked the good cakes and cookies.

"My this cake is good!" said Mr. Taylor.
"May I have some more please?"

"I will get some more cake for you,"
said Mrs. Read. "The more you buy, the more
playthings we can get for our baby room."

"My!" said Karen. "I know this social
will pay for everything we want."

"Yes, and more," said her mother.

"What are some *more* ways a church could make money to *pay* for things they need?"

65

Soon the Taylor family said they wanted
to see the new baby room.

"Who will *use* the baby room?"
"Why can't the babies be heard?"

Karen and her mother showed
them where it was.

"Look, Mother," said Judy.

"There are Mrs. White and her twins.
And Mrs. Ball and her little baby!"

"Yes," said Karen. "They are showing
everyone how we use our baby room."

"Look at Mrs. Ball's baby!" laughed Jack.
"You can see her, but you can't hear her!

And see what Mrs. White's twins are doing!
But you can't hear them!"

Help children understand that the baby room is soundproof but that
a loudspeaker broadcasts the services to the adults in the baby room.

"Now I see why you have a baby room,
laughed Mrs. Taylor.

"This way someone takes care of
the children. Then all the mothers
can come to church.

I hope we can have a baby room
in our church someday."

Mrs. Read asked, "Why not have a
social to pay for it?

We will all come and buy cake
to help pay for your baby room."

"Why would Mrs. Taylor *hope* that there could be a baby
room in her church?" How did Mrs. Read offer to help?"
"Why would a baby room be a good thing for a church to have?"
"Why isn't there a baby room in all churches?"

Places to Worship

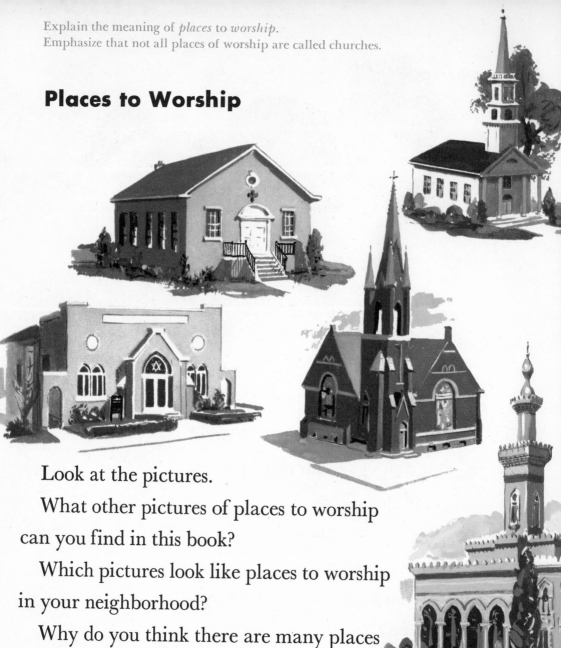

Look at the pictures.

What other pictures of places to worship can you find in this book?

Which pictures look like places to worship in your neighborhood?

Why do you think there are many places to worship in some neighborhoods?

Note other types of buildings in which people worship in pictures of other neighborhoods. Emphasize understanding that in America people can worship in the way that seems right to them.

"Find each place you have been reading about on the map."

This is a picture map of Judy's neighborhood.

Find Judy's home on the map.

Find Mr. Taylor's store.

Find the building where Mr. Ball
gets out the newspaper.

Find the school on the map.

Which is the safe way for the Taylor
children to go to school?

What can you tell about Judy's neighborhood
by reading the picture map?

Discuss each direction and question.
See "Making and Reading Maps" in "Golden Section."

Compare and contrast with the children's own neighborhood.

Mike Longway's Neighborhood

"How can you tell that Mike lives in a city neighborhood?"

Mike Longway lives in a big city.

He lives in a big, old house.

Neighborhood Fun

"Why do you think Mike is in a
wheel chair?" (Mike has had polio)

When it was hot, everyone in Mike's
neighborhood liked to get out of the house.

One hot, hot day all the neighbors were
out on the street.

The Longway family was out there, too.

Tom and Sally and the twins went
down the street.

They wanted to play ball with some
neighbor children.

But little Mike did not go. He could not
run and play like the other children.

Sally and the boys soon came back.
It was just too hot to play ball.

"What do you think the children will do now?"

Soon Mrs. Longway said, "Look, children.
Do you see what I see?

What do you think the men in that car
are going to do?"

The children looked and saw two men
jump out of the car.

When the children saw what the men
were doing, they ran down the street.

"What are the *men* doing?" (attaching
spray equipment to fire hydrant.)

Whoosh! Out came the water.

Tom ran into the water.

"Come on," he called to the others.

"Boy! how good this feels!"

Up and down they jumped.

In and out of the water they ran.

"What do you suppose Mike and *Gramps* are saying to each other?"

"In the bottom picture Mike and Gramps have *started* down the street."

Grandfather Longway looked at the children playing in the water.

Then he looked at Mike.

"Come on, Mike," he said. "You and Gramps are going to play in the water, too.

I am going to take you for a ride."

Gramps put Mike up on his back and started down the street.

"Where do you think Mike and Gramps are going?"

75

Into the water and out ran Gramps
with Mike.

"Whee!" said Mike. "That was fun!"

Back into the water ran Gramps and Mike
for another ride.

In and out, in and out.

Mike had one ride after another.

"Oh, Gramps," laughed Mike. "I could ride
like this all day long."

But Gramps had started to puff.

He puffed and puffed and puffed.

"What did Mike say that showed he enjoyed riding on Gramps' back?"
"What do you think will happen next?"

Just then the twins called to Gramps.
"We will take Mike now," said Bill.

"Come on, Mike," said Jim. "You can
ride on our backs."

"Oh, good," said Mike. "I guess
I am too big for Gramps."

Gramps laughed. "You are not
too big, Mike," he said.

"But I am too old to jump and play.
After all, I am not a jumping jack!"

The boys laughed and laughed.
They told Gramps to go on home.
And Gramps did just that. He puffed
and puffed all the way.

"Why did the children have to play in the street?"

"These pictures *show* different *kinds* of *places* to play in a city."

"After you read these two pages decide which place you liked best."

Places to Play

In some city neighborhoods, children
have to play in the street.

Other city neighborhoods have made room
for the children to play.

Where do the children play
in Mike's neighborhood?

The pictures show you some
other city neighborhoods.

Where are the children playing?

78

Where do you play in your neighborhood?

What other kinds of places to play

do you know about?

Name as many places as you can.

A Fire in the Neighborhood

The Billings and the Longways were neighbors.

One day Mrs. Billings came out and called to the Longway twins.

"Would one of you look after my children? I have to go to the store."

Jim called back, "I will! I will take good care of them for you."

Mrs. Billings went on to the store.

Jim went to take care of her four little children.

Bill went down to play in the street.

Soon he heard Jim call.

Establish the fact that the Billings and the Longways live in adjacent apartment buildings and where boys were when they *heard* Mrs. Billings call.

"What do you think Jim called to Bill?"

80

"What did Jim discover when he *got* up to the apartment?"
"What is he calling to Bill?"
"What did the twins do *right* away?"

"Bill! Bill!" called Jim.
"The building is on fire!

Come up here right away. Fast! Help me
get the children out."

Bill ran up as fast as he could.

The twins soon got the four children
out of the house.

Then Jim ran back into the building to tell
the other neighbors about the fire.

And Bill ran to call the firemen.

"What is Bill doing?"
"What do you think will happen next?"

81

This is a good time to plan a trip to neighborhood fire station, or invite a fireman or policeman to talk to children. (See "Taking Trips" in "Golden Section".)

A bell rang at the firehouse.

"When the bell *rang* at the firehouse the firemen hurried to get *their* things. Let's see what they did next."

The firemen ran to get their things.

They found out

where the fire was.

And away they went to put out the fire.

Recall location of neighborhood firehouse. Discuss sequence of action and time it will take to reach the Billings' home.

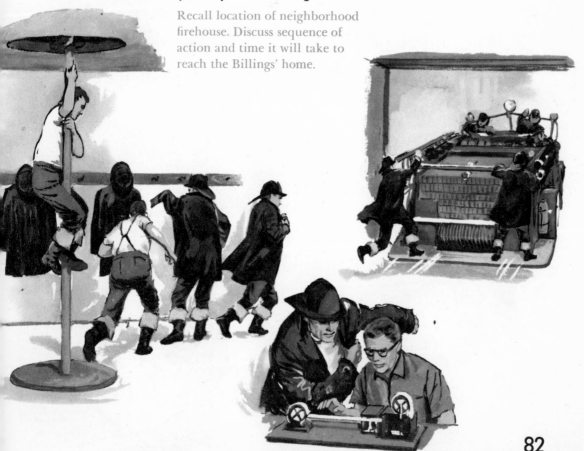

"Look at the picture. What are the firemen doing?"
"Why would the firemen have to work fast?"
"Why would the *police* want everyone to *stay* back?"

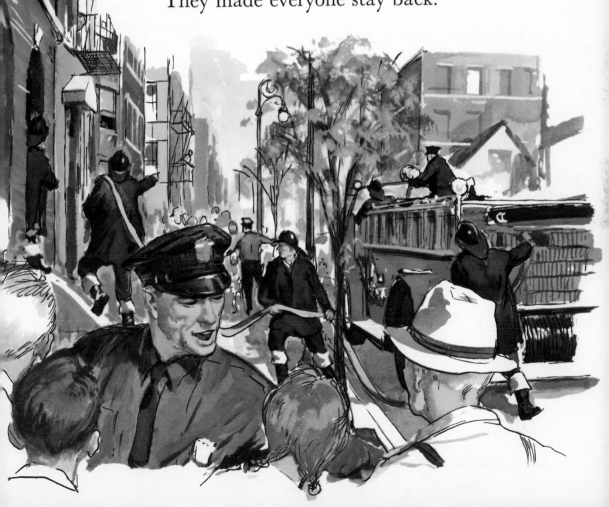

In no time at all, the firemen were
at the fire.

But the fire had a start, and the men
had to work fast.

The police were there when the firemen came.

They made everyone stay back.

As the firemen were working,
Mrs. Billings came home.

"Oh, my children!" she said.

"My children are in the building!"

One of the policemen went up to her.

"Now, now," he said. "There is no one
in that building.

I know your children are all right.
I will help you find them."

As soon as Jim saw Mrs. Billings,
he called, "Your children are all safe!

Mom and Gramps are looking after them.
I will show you where they are."

Where do you think the twins took the children so that they would be safe?
"*Where do you think* Mom *and Gramps are?*"

84

"Why were Mom and Gramps on the other side of the street?"

Jim took Mrs. Billings to her children on the other side of the street.

How happy she was to find that all her children were safe!

Then Jim said, "Mom, what will the Billings do now?

The fire was in their apartment. Where will they stay?"

"With us," said Mrs. Longway.

"Oh, no!" said Mrs. Billings.

"You do not have room for another family."

"We can make room," said Mrs. Longway.

"And we will all help you when it is safe to go back into your apartment."

"How can I thank you?" asked Mrs. Billings.

"Now, now, Mrs. Billings," said Mrs. Longway.

"After all, what are neighbors for?"

Discuss Mrs. Longway's offer and what this shows about the kind of person she is. Discuss fire-fighting in your neighborhood and generous actions of neighbors in time of trouble.

85

After the Fire

At last the fire was out. Some of the firemen
started back to the firehouse.

But some of them stayed.

They went from room to room
in the Billings apartment.

They went into other apartments
in the building looking and looking.

But the fire was all out.

Discuss the importance of checking to be sure that fire is out.

86

Firemen Protect Us

Look at the pictures.

What are the firemen doing?

How do firemen protect us?

What can you do to help keep fires from starting?

In what ways can you help when there is a fire?

87

Policemen Protect Us

What did the policemen do at the fire?

Policemen protect you and your home.

They help keep all your things safe.

The pictures show you some of the ways
that policemen protect you.

What are the policemen in each picture doing?

What are some other ways that
policemen protect you?

When should you ask a policeman for help?

Guide a discussion of the page emphasizing what
child's relationship to policemen should be.

Blue Jeans for Mike

After studying top picture locate
jeans factory on pages 70-71.
Discuss meaning of *factory*.

There is a jeans factory
in Mike's neighborhood.
Many neighbors work in the factory.
This is how the jeans are made.

Discuss sequence of making jeans.

Discuss work done in any neighborhood factory.

89

The neighbors worked all day in the factory.

Gramps worked in the factory, too. But he did not work in the daytime.

He looked after the factory at night.

All night long he went from room to room in the factory.

He had to make sure that everything was all right.

Gramps' work was like a policeman's work.

He protected the factory.

In the morning Gramps went home.

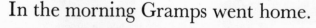

Discuss how Gramps' work is like a policeman's.

Gramps came home from work one morning
with some surprises.

He had blue jeans for Tom and the twins.

"Oh, boy, new jeans!" said Bill
when he saw the jeans. "Just what I wanted."

"Thank you, Gramps," said Tom.

"How many pairs of jeans did Gramps bring home?

Mrs. Longway saw Mike looking
at the jeans.

Let's read to find out why
he didn't bring a pair
small enough for Mike."

She could see that he wanted some, too.

So she said to Gramps, "Could you get some
jeans for Mike?"

"I don't think our jeans are made that small,"
said Gramps. "But I will see."

Establish fact that Mike's jeans
will have to be especially made.

After dinner when Gramps went to work,
he saw the man who ran the factory.

"Hello, Mr. Newman," said Gramps.

"Hello, there," said Mr. Newman.
"Did the boys like the jeans?"

"They sure did!" laughed Gramps.

"Now Mike wants jeans, too. But they
would have to be pretty small.

I guess you don't make jeans that small."

"No, we don't," said Mr. Newman.

"But we will see what we can do.
You find out just how small Mike's jeans
would have to be."

"I will do just that," said Gramps.
"Thank you, Mr. Newman."

"What do you think Mr. Newman plans to do?"

In the morning Gramps told Mom
what Mr. Newman had said.

Mom said, "I know how to make sure that
Mike's jeans will be small enough."

"What is Mom doing to make sure that
Mike's jeans will be small *enough?*"

"How many *women* are working on Mike's jeans?"

The next day at the factory,
one of the women made Mike's jeans.

"What was different about the way Mike's jeans were made?"

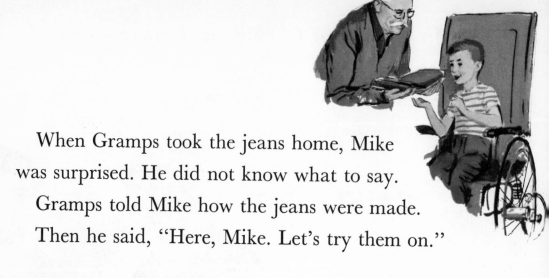

When Gramps took the jeans home, Mike
was surprised. He did not know what to say.
Gramps told Mike how the jeans were made.
Then he said, "Here, Mike. Let's try them on."

He helped Mike get into his jeans.
They were just right!
"Now," said Mike, "I look like
the big boys, don't I?" Discuss Mike's reaction to his new jeans.
Tom said, "You sure do. Your jeans
are just like ours." Note Mike's appearance on crutches.
"Not just like yours," said Mike.
"My jeans were made just for me."

Many Things Are Made

"There was a bakery and a *chair* factory in Mike's neighborhood."

Food is made in this big factory.

What food do you see that you like?

Name some other kinds of food

that are made in a factory.

Do some people in your neighborhood

help make the food you eat?

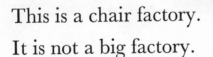

This is a chair factory.

It is not a big factory.

Just one kind of chair is made here.

Do you have a chair like this in your home?

Is there a factory in your neighborhood

where things for your home are made?

95   Discuss factory-made food and household items such as chairs.

Big airplanes are made

in this airplane factory.

It takes many people to make

just one airplane.

What other things to ride in

are made in a factory?

Toy airplanes and other kinds of toys

are made in this factory.

What toy do you have that was

made in a factory?

Compare and contrast the toy
factory and airplane factory.

Is there a factory in your neighborhood?

What other kind of factory

do you know about?

Discuss factories located in your neighborhood.
Discuss work members of children's families
do in factories.

What is made there?

Neighborhood House

Down the street from the Longways

was a big Neighborhood House.

Everyone in the neighborhood

liked to go there.

Tom liked to go there to make baskets.

He was learning to make toys, too.

Sally liked to go there and dance.

The twins played basketball there.

Mike liked to paint pictures.

Discuss any similar
facilities in child's own
neighborhood.

97

"What do you do on *Saturdays*? What *games* do you like to play?"

Mrs. Small helped everyone
who came to Neighborhood House.

One Saturday she saw the Longway children.

"Hello," she said. "I have news for you.

We are going to have a show
next Saturday night.

Discuss what Mrs. Small does at Neighborhood House and what she is saying to the children.

Let's get the other children and find out
what each one can do for the show."

Soon everyone was talking about the show.

Jim said, "Let's have a basketball game.
Maybe the boys could play the fathers."

"That would be fun!" said Mrs. Small.

Sally said, "We girls could dance."

Tom said, "Some of us can show people
how we make baskets and toys."

"What would you like to do for such a show as the one being planned?"

"I will paint a picture
for the show," said Mike.

"What kind of picture do you think Mike will make?"

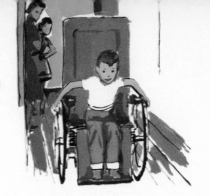

"Do you suppose Mike finished his picture by *noon*? Let's see how long it took him to finish his picture."

Mike went right to the painting room
in his chair. He worked all morning long
on a big picture.

At noon Mike and all
the other children went home.

After lunch they came back
to Neighborhood House.

They worked all afternoon.

When it was time to go home for dinner,
Mike took his picture to Mrs. Small.

"Who do you think will come to the show?"

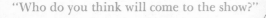

Note that show at Neighborhood House
is held on following Saturday.
Discuss people who came to the show.
"What have some of the children made?"

The next Saturday night just about
everyone in the neighborhood
went to the show.

First Tom took his family to the room
where the baskets and toys were made.

He showed them a toy airplane
that he had made.

Next the Longways went to see Sally
and some other little girls dance.

It was a very beautiful dance.

100

Then came the basketball game.

The fathers played the best they could, but the boys were too fast for them.

The fathers lost the game.

After the game, Gramps looked at Mike.

"Say, Mike, what did you do for the show?" he asked.

"I painted a picture," said Mike.

"It may not be very good, but it is the very best I could do.

Would you and Mom like to see it?"

"We sure would, Mike," said Gramps. "Let's go."

So Mom and Gramps took Mike to the painting room in his chair.

How surprised everyone was to see the picture that Mike had painted.

Mike had a surprise, too.

"What do you think the surprise will be?"

101

"Which part of the show did you think was best?"

On Mike's picture it said "FIRST PRIZE!"

"I thought you said your picture was
not very good," said Mom. "But look, Mike.
Your picture got first prize."

"First prize?" was all Mike could say.

Just then Mrs. Small came in.

"Oh, here you are, Mike," she said.
"Look what I have for you.

We think your picture is the best thing
anyone made for our show.

So you get first prize!"

This time Mike could not say a thing.

He just looked at his prize.

"See if you can decide why Mike couldn't say anything when he found out he got first prize."

Discuss importance of Neighborhood House to Mike's neighborhood.

This is a picture map of Mike's neighborhood.

Find where the Longways and

the Billings live.

How is this picture *map* different from the picture made *by* Mike? Help children locate important places on picture map as suggested by the text.

Find the firehouse.

Find the factory where Gramps works.

Find Neighborhood House.

What can you tell about Mike's neighborhood

by reading the picture map?

See "Making and Reading Maps" in the "Golden Section".

Compare and contrast with the children's own neighborhood.

Linda West's Neighborhood

Linda West lives in this neighborhood.
Her home is in an apartment building.

At the Store.

Linda was playing with some girls
back of her apartment building.

"Linda, will you please come here?"
called her mother.

"Oh, Mother," Linda called back.

"Do I have to come now?
We are just going to have a party."

"I know, dear," said her mother.
"But I want you to go to the store for me.
I do not have time to go."

"Here I am, Mother," called Linda
when she went into the apartment.

"What do you want me to get at the store?"

"Store, store," Linda's little brother Bobby said.
"I want to go."

"Oh, Mother, no," said Linda. "You know how
he gets into everything at the store."

"Store, store," said Bobby.
"Please, Linda, please!"

"Oh, Mother, does he have to go?" asked Linda.

"I know just how you feel," said her mother,
"but I have to get dinner now.

Please take Bobby with you."

"Oh, dear!" said Linda. "Come on, Bobby."

So away they went to the store.

107   *"How did Linda feel about taking Bobby to the store?"*

"Why did Linda use a *cart* at the store?"

"She had to get milk and *bread*. What else do you think she had to get?"

"Why do you think Linda let Bobby push the cart?"

At the store Linda said, "We will take this cart, Bobby.

We will get the things Mother wants and put them in the cart.

You can make the cart go. I will tell you where to stop."

When they came to the milk, Linda said, "Stop here, Bobby."

Linda put some milk into the cart.

"Milk, milk," said Bobby. He put some milk into the cart, too.

But Linda was not looking at Bobby.

"What did Linda stop to put in the cart?"

"Do you think Bobby will put other things into the cart?"

Soon Linda said, "Bobby, stop the cart here.
We must get some bread."

Linda put the bread into the cart.

"Bread, bread. See, Linda," said Bobby.

And he put some bread into the cart.

But Linda was looking at some cookies.

She did not hear what her brother said.

She did not see what he did.

Linda put some cookies into the cart and
she and Bobby went on.

109   "After Linda put the bread into the cart, what did Bobby do?"

"Why didn't Linda hear what Bobby said?"

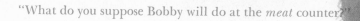

"What do you suppose Bobby will do at the *meat* counter?"

"How did Linda know what kind of meat to get?"

"We have the milk and bread,"
said Linda. "And we have the cookies.

Now we will get the meat."

A man who worked there said,
"Hello, Linda. What can I do for you?"

It was Linda's neighbor, Mr. Downing.

"Hello, Mr. Downing," said Linda. "Please
read this. It tells what meat my mother wants."

Soon Linda had the meat.

"Now, I have everything," she said.

But when Linda put the meat into the cart,
she saw what Bobby had put into it.

"How did all this get in our cart?"
she asked.

"I helped," said Bobby.

"Why did Bobby put the extra things in the cart?"
"What do you think Linda will do now?"

110

"Oh, Bobby West!" said Linda.

"Now I have to put everything back."

One at a time, Linda took out the things
that Bobby had put into the cart.
She took them all back.
When Linda was not looking,   "Do you think she will remember
Bobby put the meat back, too.   to *pay* for what she bought?"

Linda went to pay for the things
in her cart.
Then Bobby helped her take them home.

"What do you think will happen when Linda's mother cannot find the meat?"

"Here we are, Mother," Linda called.

"And here is everything you wanted."

"Thank you, Linda," said her mother.

But when Mrs. West put the things away, she asked, "Where is the meat?"

"It must be there, Mother," said Linda.

"Mr. Downing had just what you wanted. What could have happened to it?"

Linda looked and Mrs. West looked. They could not find the meat. It was not there.

"Why do you think Bobby didn't say what *happened* at the store?"

"Do you think Linda will have to go back to the store?"

Dear Tom,
    This is the way I looked
when I was in the hospital.
    We are sorry you are hurt.
We hope you will be back soon.
    When you come back,
we will play that it is
your birthday.
We will sing what you want
to sing.
We will do all the things
you want to do.
            Happy Birthday
            Mrs. Little

At last the letters were all ready.

"What do you think Jim is asking the man at the *stamp window?*"

At the post office, Mrs. Little said,
"Here, Jim. You may buy the stamps."

Jim went to the man at the stamp window.

"My, what a big letter!" said the man.

"It will take ten stamps."

"This is not just one letter," said Jim.
"All our letters are in here.

The letters are for Tom Peters. He is
in the hospital."

"It is his birthday," said Linda.
"We want Tom to get our letters today."

"Then you will want this stamp too,"
said the man. "Put it on your letter.

Then your letter will go
to the hospital right away."

The boys put all the stamps
on the letter.

And soon the letter was on its way to Tom.

"Have you ever seen a letter or package with this kind of stamp?"
Discuss use of special delivery.

That was a long day for Tom in the hospital.

It was not like a birthday at all.

All day long he thought about what he would
be doing at school.

At last he went to sleep.

Soon after Tom went to sleep, a nurse
came into his room.

"A big letter for Tom Peters!"
she called. "This is no time to sleep!"

Tom looked up in surprise.
"A letter for me?" he said.

Tom had fun reading all
the birthday letters.

He laughed at Mrs. Little's
funny picture.

He showed the letters
to the other children in the room.

Tom showed the letters to Doctor Fellman
when he came in.

"What was Tom doing when he got his letter?"
"What do you think will happen next?"

Then Tom's mother came to see him.

She had birthday surprises for him, too.

She had a big birthday cake.

All the children in the room had
some of Tom's birthday cake.

Doctor Fellman and the nurses had some, too.

There was enough for everyone.

The boy next to Tom said, "Say, Tom!
If you had to get hurt, I am glad
you were here on your birthday."

"This is a good place to be when you
are hurt," said Tom. "And I have had
a good birthday after all.

But best of all, I am going to have
another birthday when I go back to school."

"Was there *enough* cake for everyone?"
"What things helped Tom have a good time at the hospital?"

This is a good time to plan a visit to the post office.
See "Extending Experiences" in *Guidebook* and "Taking Trips" in "Golden
Section" for suggestions.

Mail in the Neighborhood

Many people in the post office
helped get the letter to Tom.

"These next pages show what the *men* in the
post office did to get the letter to
Tom and how the *mail* gets to other
people in a neighborhood."

Some men did this.

Then a man did this.

And the stamps looked like this.

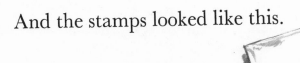

133

These pictures show what happened next
to the children's letter.

Review the sequence of what
happened to Tom's letter.

All letters do not go as fast as Tom's did.

These pictures show what happens

to some letters.

What are the people in each picture doing?

Where do you mail letters?

How does the mail come to your house?

How can you help people who work

in the post office?

135

"The children in Linda's neighborhood knew the song, *God Bless America*. Where do you think they learned it?"

The Neighborhood Sing

Identify Mr. *Nicoli* and refer to pages 104-105 for location of shop.

All the children in the neighborhood

liked Mr. Nicoli. He was their friend.

They liked to see him work on their shoes.

They liked to hear him sing.

Mr. Nicoli liked the children, too.

When they came to the door, he would

laugh and say, "Come in! Come in!

Come in, my little friends!"

Then Mr. Nicoli would sing

as he went on with his work.

Soon someone would say, "Please sing

about America, Mr. Nicoli."

Then Mr. Nicoli would say, "But you,

my little friends, must sing, too."

So the children would sing with him.

They liked that best of all.

One day Doctor Fellman came in when some
of the children were singing.

They were singing "God Bless America."

"Why that is beautiful!" he said.

"How did you children learn to sing
'God Bless America' like that?"

"Mr. Nicoli helped us," said Linda.

"All the children in the neighborhood
know 'God Bless America,'" said Tom.

"That they do," said Mr. Nicoli.

"I would like to hear all of you sing,"
said Doctor Fellman.

"But we can't all sing here. Mr. Nicoli's
store is too little," said Linda.

"There must be a place big enough
for everyone to sing," said Doctor Fellman.

"Where do you think the children in Linda's
neighborhood might go to sing?"
"Let's read the next page and see if Doctor
Fellman found a place big enough
for all the children to sing."

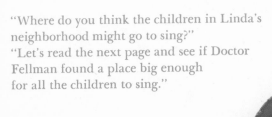

Refer to pages 104-105 and locate the *park* where the sing was to be held.

So Doctor Fellman talked with some
of his friends in the neighborhood.

They all said that they would like to hear
Mr. Nicoli and the children sing.

They thought it would be fun to have
a neighborhood sing.

But no one could think of a place
that was big enough.

Then Mr. West said, "I know. Why not have
our sing in the neighborhood park?"

"Dollman Park would be just the place,"
said Mr. Peters. "How about a letter
to each family to tell them about it?"

"Good. We can write the letter now,"
said Mr. Downing.

Soon every family in the neighborhood
got one of the letters.

Do you like to sing?

Come to the Neighborhood Sing

Come and sing with your neighbors

Dollman Park - 7:00 next Saturday night

On Saturday night, many, many people
came to the park.

As soon as everyone was there,
Mr. West began to talk.

"Friends and neighbors," he said.
"We are glad to see you here. This sing is
something new in our neighborhood.

It all began when Doctor Fellman heard
some children singing at Mr. Nicoli's.

And now here is Mr. Nicoli who is going
to help us all sing."

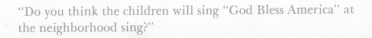

Then Mr. Nicoli got up and began to sing.
And everyone began to sing with him.

Sometimes just the men sang.

Sometimes just the women sang.

Sometimes everyone sang, men, women,
and children.

"Do you think the children will sing "God Bless America" at
the neighborhood sing?"

It was just about time to go home when
Mr. Nicoli said, "Come, my little friends.
Now you must sing for everyone."

Then just the boys and girls sang
with Mr. Nicoli.
They all sang "God Bless America."
"That was beautiful!" said Mrs. Peters.
"Please sing it again," said Mrs. Little.
"We will, we will!" said Mr. Nicoli.
"But this time, everyone must sing."
So everyone sang "God Bless America."
"Beautiful, beautiful!" said Mr. Nicoli.
"You sing as good as the people
in my old country.
We must do this again."

Develop the understanding that singing "God Bless America" is one way people
show they love their country.
Let the children sing "God Bless America" as they think the children
in the neighborhood sang it.

Good Times in Your Park

"Read the page and be ready to answer the questions."

Linda's neighbors had many good times in their park.

What are they doing in the pictures?

Is there a park in your neighborhood?

Do you do these same things at your park?

Which of these things do your neighbors do?

What do you like to do best?

What have you learned in your park?

Who helps you play and have fun in your park?

How can you help everyone have fun in your park?

See lesson plan in *Guidebook*.
"In Linda's neighborhood there are many different *sounds* to hear.
What sounds can you hear in our neighborhood if you *listen* carefully?"

Looking and Listening

In Linda's neighborhood there are
beautiful things to see.

There are beautiful sounds to hear.

Looking and listening helps us
learn many things.

Look for things in your neighborhood
that you think are beautiful.

Listen for sounds that you think
are beautiful.

Be ready to tell about the things
you see and the sounds you hear.

Make pictures of some
of the beautiful things you have seen.

Can you make some of the sounds
you have heard in your neighborhood?

Make a picture of what you see as you
listen to some of the sounds in your neighborhood.

Hospital

Library

Dollman Park

Post Office

School

Church

Store

Peters

Downing

Nicoli

West

This is a picture map of Linda's neighborhood.

Find the apartment house where Linda lives.

Which way did Linda go to get to the store?

Which way did she go to the library?

Find the school and the post office.

Which way did the children go to mail

the letter to Tom?

What can you tell about Linda's neighborhood

by reading the picture map?

"How is the picture *map* of Linda's neighborhood different from the big picture
of it you have seen?" (labels)

See "Making and Reading Maps" in "Golden Section".

Compare and contrast Steve's new neighborhood with children's own neighborhood.

Steve Bell's New Neighborhood

The Bell family is moving
to this new neighborhood.

"Into which house do you think Steve Bell's family is moving?"

Moving Day

"Has your family ever moved?"
"What did the moving *men* do?"
"What did you do?"
Identify members of Bell family.

Moving day was a busy day
for the Bell family.

They were moving to a new neighborhood.

Everyone in the family helped.

Everyone but Dick.

He was too little to help. So he was
at Grandmother Bell's house.

Steve helped Father take
the little things out of the house.

Patty and Mother helped the moving men.

The Bell's dog was busy, too.

He ran in and out. In and out!

He was busy, but he was no help at all!

"Read the page to see what Steve and Father did after the moving men put the last things into the *van*."

Soon the moving men had put
the last big things into the moving van.

Father and Steve had put
the last little thing into the car.

Just then out ran the Bell's dog.

"Here, boy," said Steve.

"Get into the car."

Then back to the house went
Father and Steve.

Father looked about the house and said,
"We have everything. Now we can go.
Come, Mother, come Patty!"

Then they went out to the car.

Away went the moving van.

Away went the Bell family.

"Which started first, the moving van or the Bells' car?"

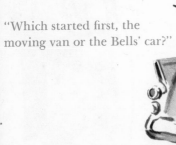

147

On the way to the new neighborhood,
Steve said, "Stop the car!

We forgot something!"

But Father did not stop.

"Oh, Father, stop!" said Patty.
"We forgot Smokey!"

"That dog!" said Father. "When I saw
Smokey last, he was in the car."

"I know he was," said Steve. "But he
is not here now."

"We will have to go back," said Mother.

"Oh, yes," said Father. "But what a time
for Smokey to get lost! On moving day!"

So the Bells went all the way back
to the old house.

And there was Smokey!

How happy he was to see the family!

"Get in, Smokey," said Father. "Now we
do have everything.

We can go to our new house."

Then on to the new neighborhood
went the Bells.

*"Why did the moving men happen to
get to the new house first?"*

"There is our new house," said Steve.

"Look!" said Patty. "The moving men
are here first."

"Oh, I did not want that
to happen," said Mother.

"I must go and tell the men
where to put things."

"Patty, you go on in with your mother,"
said Father. "Steve and I will take the
things out of the car."

149
"What do you think will happen now?"

Mother and Patty went to the house.

Steve helped Father take things

out of the car.

"Here, Steve," said Father.

"Take this picture into the house."

Just then Steve saw Patty.

"Here comes Patty on the run," he said.

"What could have happened now?" asked Father.

Patty said, "Mother wants you to help her.

The moving men put all our things

in the house next to ours."

"Oh, no!" said Father.

Just then Smokey ran out of the car.

"Put that dog back in the car, Steve,

and take care of things here," said Father.

"I must go and see what I can do."

"Get in the car, Smokey," said Steve.

"And see if you can stay there this time!

We have work to do and you get

in everyone's way."

150

"How long do you think it took to put everything in the *right* house?"
Discuss sequence of events and discuss how the trouble might have been avoided.
"What do you suppose Steve *told* his grandmother?"

At last everything was in the right house.

The moving men were just going away
when Grandmother Bell came with Dick.

"Here we are!" she said. "We came
to see the new house."

Steve told what had happened when the
family had to go back for Smokey.

Grandmother Bell laughed and laughed!

"Oh, Smokey!" she said. "You are a good dog,
but a dog is no help on moving day!"

Building a New Neighborhood

Many men worked to build
the new neighborhood.

They used big machines to help them
do the work.

"How are machines being *used* in building the new neighborhood?"
"What kind of work have you seen men doing with big *machines*?"

What did the men use the big machines
to do?

What work did they do
without big machines?

What other work must someone do
before the houses are ready to live in?

Discuss the sequence of work shown in the pictures.
Relate to other kinds of work that must be
done before the houses are ready to live in.

153

Some men worked to make streets.

They used big machines and trucks
to help them do the work.

The men made good streets
for the neighborhood.

Then men came to work in the yards.

They used trucks and machines, too.

Soon the yards were ready.

But they were not beautiful yards.

What must each family do
to make the yards beautiful?

New Friends

"Steve and Patty *hope* that the family next door has some children. Do you think they do?"

"Mother, Mother! Look!" said Steve.

"A family is moving into that new house next door."

"Oh, good!" said Mother. "Now we will have neighbors.

Run and ask them if we can help."

"I hope they have some boys I can play with," said Steve.

"How is the moving van different from the one used to move the Bells' things?" (cross-country van)

"And girls for me!" said Patty.

156

The moving men were busy moving
things into the house.

Steve and Patty saw a mother and
father in the house.

But they did not see children.

"Say, Patty," said Steve. "Why don't
you go and see if they have some boys?"

"Why don't you?" said Patty. "I don't
care about boys. I hope they have girls."

"I just don't feel like it," said Steve.

So Patty and Steve just looked
at the other house.

"Steve and Patty *hear* something as they sit talking. What do you think they heard?"

Soon Patty asked, "Oh, Steve, did you hear something? Is that Smokey?"

"Yes, it is," said Steve. "Don't you know our Smokey when you hear him?"

Just then they saw Smokey. He had a boy with him.

"Look," said Patty. "Smokey has found a boy for you to play with."

"Hello," said Steve to the new boy.

But Smokey's new friend just looked at Patty and Steve.

Then Steve said, "I am Steve Bell, and this is my sister, Patty.

What is your name?"

The new boy just looked at them.

Then he ran away.

Smokey ran, too.

"Why do you think the little boy did not talk to Steve and Patty?"

158

Steve and Patty ran next door
to find Smokey's new friend.

Two boys came to the door.

"Hello," said Patty. "We live next door.
We are Patty and Steve Bell."

"Come in," said one of the boys. "I am
Jack Vanstreet, and this is my brother, Tom.

This is our mother and father."

"Was that your little boy playing
with our dog, Mrs. Vanstreet?" asked Steve.

"Yes," said Mrs. Vanstreet. "He used to live
in another country. But he is going to be
our little boy now."

"Why can't he talk?" asked Steve.

"Oh, Peter can talk," said Mrs. Vanstreet.
"He talks like everyone does in the country
where he used to live.

He will soon learn to talk the way you do."

"Come on," said Tom. "We will go and
find Peter."

159

"Peter *started* to run away again but something
happened to stop him. What do you think it was?"

The children found Peter playing
with Smokey in the back yard.

When he saw Patty and Steve, Peter
started to run away.

"Please stay here, Peter," said Patty.
"We want to be your friends."

Peter did not know what Patty said.
But he could feel that she wanted
to be his friend.

"Look at me, Peter," said Tom Vanstreet.
"Say Hello."

"Say Hello, Peter," said Patty.

Peter looked at Tom. He looked at Jack.

He looked at Smokey.

He looked at Steve and Patty.

At last he laughed and said, "Hello, Peter!"

"How could Peter tell that Patty wanted
to be his friend? Do you think he knew
what Patty was saying?"

Discuss experiences children
may have had with someone who
spoke another language.

See "Extending Experiences"
in *Guidebook* lesson plan.

A New Home in a New Country

In his country, Peter lived
with his father and mother.
He lived in a pretty little house.
His home was like yours in many ways.
He went to school and to church.
He lived in a neighborhood.
Why do you think he came
to our country?
What do you think Peter would like
to know about America?
What could Steve and his friends do
to make Peter feel at home?
If you went to live in another country,
how would you want children there to help you?
What would you like to know
about the children in that country?
Are there children in your neighborhood
who came from another country?
What would you like to ask them?

Capitalize on the different cultural backgrounds of your class during the discussion.

Moving Things from Place to Place

Men with big moving vans helped
the Bells and the Vanstreets.

The pictures show other ways of moving
things from one place to another.

Which ways are used in your neighborhood?

Name some other ways of moving things
from one place to another.

Ways to Ride from Place to Place

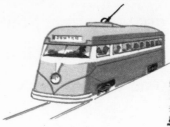

In Steve's neighborhood, some people
ride to work on a bus.

Some of them go in cars.

In what other ways do people ride to work?

People can go to many places in a bus.

Some children ride to school
in a school bus.

Where could you go on a bus?

How do the children ride to your school?

In what other ways can people ride
from one place to another?

How do you think Peter came to America?

Which ways could take many people
at one time?

Working Together

"Where are you going, Steve?"
asked Mr. Bell. "I want you to help me."

"I was going to help the Vanstreets,"
said Steve.

"They are going to get some trees
for the yard. But if we don't go right away,
the machines will have the trees all down."

"That is just what I am going to do,"
said Father. "Mr. Vanstreet told me
about the trees."

Just then, Patty, Dick, and Mother came out.

"We are all ready," said Mother. "I hope
we can find a beautiful tree for our back yard.
And I want four little trees for the doorway."

"Why do you think the Bells and other neighbors want to get trees?"
"Where do you think they will go to get the trees?"

Before long the Bells saw the place
where they were going to get the trees.

Men with big machines were about to take
the trees up to make room for new houses.

Locate the wooded area on pages 144-145.

Many of the Bell's neighbors were there.

They all wanted trees for their yards.

Steve said, "Here come the Vanstreets
and Peter."

"Oh, Steve," said Patty. "Peter is a
Vanstreet, too."

"No, he is not," said Steve. "He can't
talk like a Vanstreet."

"Maybe he can't," said Patty. "But
he is a Vanstreet.

And he is learning to talk the way
we all do. I am teaching him."

165

Discuss what Patty is *teaching* Peter.
Compare and contrast the attitude of Patty and Steve toward their neighbor, Peter Vanstreet.

Mr. Vanstreet and Mr. Bell went right
to work on a tree.

But it was too big for two men
to get it up.

Three neighbors came to help them.

Before long the men had the tree up.

They put it in Mr. Vanstreet's truck.

Then they looked for another tree
for Mr. Bell.

Just then they saw Steve's Uncle David
and Aunt Susan.

They wanted trees for their yard, too.

So together the men looked for a tree
for Uncle David's yard.

Aunt Susan went to find Mrs. Bell.

All the men worked together and each one
helped the other.

"How did the neighbor men
help each other?"

166

All this time, the mothers and the girls were looking for little trees.

Everyone was so busy that they forgot about Dick.

But not Peter. He saw Dick.

Dick was trying to get a little tree up.

It was just a little stick, but Dick could not get it up.

Peter did not say a thing. He just went to try to help Dick.

Before long Peter and Dick had the little tree up.

Then they found another little tree, and another, and another.

They took the four little trees to the Bell's car.

Then they found four other little trees and took them to the Vanstreet's truck.

"Why do you think Peter helped Dick?"
"What does this tell you about Peter?"

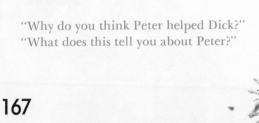

When the Bells and the Vanstreets came
back to their cars, they saw all the trees.

"Now where did all these little trees
come from?" asked Mrs. Vanstreet.

Just then Peter and Dick came back.
They each had another little tree.
That made ten little trees they had found!

"Now we know where the trees came from,"
laughed Mrs. Bell.

"I guess Peter is all right," said Steve.

"Maybe he can't talk like we do, but
he does know how to work."

"Yes," said Patty. "And Peter knows how
to talk, too! You just listen, Steve Bell!"

Then Patty looked at Peter.

"What is your name, Peter?" she asked.

Peter looked at Patty and said,
"My name is Peter Vanstreet."

Neighbors Work Together

Discuss how the Bells and the Van-streets have improved the appearance of their houses. (Compare with pages 144-145.)

Think how Steve's neighborhood looked before moving day.

The picture shows how people worked to make it beautiful.

What do people in your neighborhood do to make it beautiful?

Neighbors Play Together

All the children in Steve's neighborhood
had fun playing together.

Steve and the Vanstreet boys liked
to play games with the other boys.

Sometimes just the big boys
played together.

Sometimes big and little boys
played together.

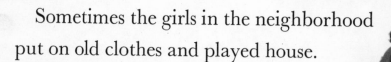

Sometimes the girls in the neighborhood
put on old clothes and played house.

Sometimes the boys and girls
played together.

How do you and your friends
play together?

Compare and contrast the way children are
playing together with the way children
in your neighborhood play together.

Christmas in the New Neighborhood

"Br-r-r!" said Mrs. Bell.
"My, but it is good to be home!
Patty, why is Dick up, too?"

"He wanted to hear what happened
at the meeting," said Patty.

"Tell us, tell us," said Steve.

"Oh, it was a good meeting," said Mother.
"We neighbors talked about Christmas."

"Yes," said Father. "And what a
Christmas this is going to be!"

"What do you think the neighbors decided at the meeting?"

"What are we going to do?" asked Steve.

"We are going to make this neighborhood into a fairyland by Christmas," said Mother.

"A Christmas fairyland?" said Patty.

"Oh, Mother! How can we help?"

"There are many ways you can help," said Father. "There will be enough work for everyone to do."

Mother said, "Now let's get busy and think of what the Bell family can do."

The next day every family
in the neighborhood was busy.

Some people put lights on Christmas
trees in their yards.

Some put many lights on their homes.

Many people made their doorways
look like Christmas.

The children made beautiful things
to put on the Christmas trees.

Everyone helped make the neighborhood
into a Christmas fairyland.

Everyone in the neighborhood was busy.
The next day, the next, and the next!

There were surprises to make and hide.

There were Christmas plays at school,
and Christmas music at church.

Christmas was a happy, busy time
for everyone.

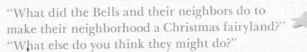

"What did the Bells and their neighbors do to
make their neighborhood a Christmas fairyland?"
"What else do you think they might do?"

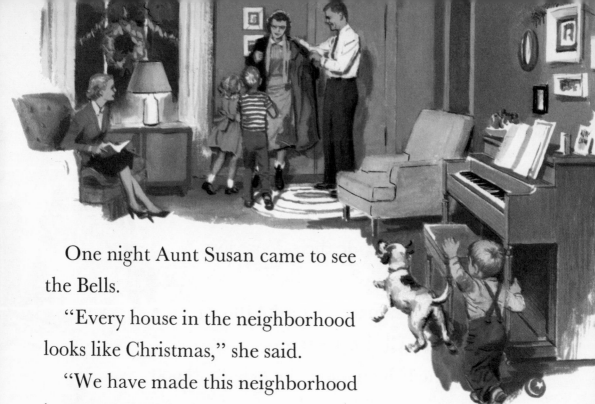

One night Aunt Susan came to see the Bells.

"Every house in the neighborhood looks like Christmas," she said.

"We have made this neighborhood into a Christmas fairyland.

But I just came from the Children's Hospital. It does not look like Christmas in the hospital."

"What could we do?" asked Patty.

"We could get some trees and lights for the rooms," said Father.

Steve said, "And Patty and I could make things to put on the trees."

"But all the children in the neighborhood will want to do something," said Patty.

"Aunt Susan has just come from the Children's *Hospital.* "Why do you suppose she is coming to see the Bells?"

"What do you think the children will do?"

174

"What could we children do?" asked Steve.

"I know," said Patty. "We could all sing carols at the hospital."

Aunt Susan said, "The children there would like that."

"Oh, Mother," said Patty. "Could everyone come to our house to work on the carols?"

"Yes," said her mother. "Father knows all the Christmas carols. He will help."

"And I will get some of the other fathers to help, too," said Mr. Bell.

All the children in the neighborhood came to the Bell house the next night. They had fun singing the carols.

"What Christmas carols could you sing?"

175

The day before Christmas, the neighbors
met at the Bell house.

Each one had something for the children
in the hospital.

They had trees and lights for their rooms.

They had surprises to open and
many good things to eat.

Then away they all went to the hospital.

At the hospital, the children went
up and down the halls singing carols.

Some of the children in the hospital
began to sing with them.

The fathers and mothers put up
the trees and lights.

Then the children opened their surprises.

Christmas had come to the Children's Hospital!

"When did everyone go to the Children's Hospital?"
"What did the children in the hospital do?"

When the children went back home,
they sang carols for all the neighbors.

"Our neighborhood does look like a
Christmas fairyland," said Steve.

"And best of all," said Patty, "it feels
like Christmas!"

Steve said, "This kind of Christmas makes
me feel good all over!"

"What do you like best about Christmas?"
"What two important things did the people in Steve's neighborhood do at Christmas time?"

Compare with pages 144-145.
Discuss why the *shopping center* looks like a fairyland.

Christmas in the New Shopping Center

The Bell's new neighborhood had a
big shopping center.

Everyone at the shopping center had worked
to make it look like a Christmas fairyland, too.

There were trees and lights and
other beautiful things.

And in the center was a big, big
Christmas tree with many, many lights.

The feeling of Christmas was everywhere!

Where do the people in your neighborhood
do their Christmas shopping?

What do the people in your neighborhood
do at Christmas time?

What do they do to make the neighborhood
beautiful at other times of the year?

Do you like Christmas time or some other
time of the year best? Why?

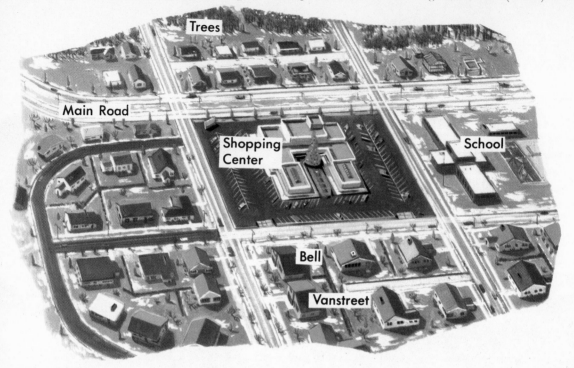

This is a picture map of Steve's neighborhood.

Find the Bell house.

Find the school.

How would the Bell children go to school?

How would the Bells go to the shopping center?

Name all the other places you see

in this picture map of the new neighborhood.

What can you tell about Steve's new neighborhood

by reading the picture map?

Identify locations as suggested in text and compare with pages 144-145.
Compare and contrast with features of landscapes in your own neighborhood.
See "Making and Reading Maps" in "Golden Section".

Your Own Neighborhood

own, winter, spring, summer, most, often, plants, flag.

This year you have learned how people
live and work together in neighborhoods.

All year long you have learned more
and more about your own neighborhood.

You have seen it in fall, in winter,
and as it is now.

You have seen the homes, yards, trees,
and gardens in your neighborhood.

You have seen the buildings where people
work or go to have fun.

You have seen people working, playing,
and going from place to place.

You have seen old things and new things.

Now you are ready to make a book
about your own neighborhood.

Then you can show your family
what you have learned.

Name your book "My Own Neighborhood."

Start your book by telling where you live.

Fall, Winter, Spring, and Summer

Try to think how your neighborhood looked when school began last fall.

What happened to the trees, yards, gardens, or fields in the fall?

What happened when winter came?

Make a picture to show what work your neighbors do outdoors in winter.

How can you tell when it is spring?

Make pictures to show work that your neighbors do in spring.

Tell what you do to have fun in spring.

Tell what you do on very hot summer days.

Tell what your neighbors do in summer.

Make pictures to show work that your neighbors do in their yards in summer.

At what time of the year would you see people with umbrellas?

In your book tell why you like fall, winter, spring, or summer best.

Places to Learn

Make a picture of your school
for your book.

Put the name of your school on your picture.

Tell about three other places where
you can learn to do new things.

Tell what you could learn at each place.

Places to Worship

Now think about the places to worship
in your neighborhood.

Paint a picture for your book of the one
that you like the best.

Beautiful Things

Tell about beautiful things that you have
seen or heard in your neighborhood.

Which do you think are the most beautiful?
Tell why you think so in your book.

Make a picture of the most beautiful
thing in your neighborhood.

Neighborhood Fun

Everyone does not like to have fun
in the same way.

Some people like to play games.

Some people like to go to ball games.

Some people like to go to the park.

Others like to see moving pictures.

Some people like to read or look at TV.

Some people like to sing, or paint, or dance.

What do you think is the most fun to do?

What games do you often play when
you can't go out?

What games do you play most often
with your friends?

What games do you play most often
with your family?

In your book tell where children go to play
together in your neighborhood.

Make pictures for your book to show what
children do to have fun in your neighborhood.

Things That Are Raised or Made

Make pictures for your book of some plants and animals in your neighborhood.

Make a picture to show someone planting one kind of plant that people eat.

Tell when people do this planting.

Tell how one plant or animal is used by your family.

Tell about something that is made in your neighborhood.

Tell what you can buy in your neighborhood stores.

Neighborhood Rules

Why don't all neighborhoods have the same rules?

Which of the rules in your neighborhood do you think are the best ones?

Tell how you can show that you are a good neighbor.

From Place to Place

Put pictures in your book of trucks
that you often see in your neighborhood.

Name three other ways that things
are taken from place to place.

What ways do people in your neighborhood
use most often to ride from place to place?

Make pictures to show ways to ride
that take many people at one time.

Ways of Telling Something to Others

Try to think of ways you have told things
to others and have learned things from them.

What could you put in your book
about telephones and newspapers?

Tell four things you have learned
from moving pictures and TV.

Write or show in pictures what you have
learned about mail in your neighborhood.

People Who Protect Us

What can you put in your book about the work of the people in these pictures?

Name some people you have met who do each kind of work.

What other people help protect you and your neighbors?

What do these people do to keep your neighborhood safe?

What could happen if there was no one to do this kind of work?

Make pictures of three things you could do to help keep your neighborhood safe.

Our Country's Flag

On what days have you seen many flags in your neighborhood?

In your book, name two places where you could see the flag every school day.

Did you put a flag in the picture you painted of your school?

Put a picture of our country's flag in your book.

People from Other Places

Are there people in your neighborhood who came from another place in America?

Do you know someone who came from another country?

What have you learned this year about some other country?

What would you like to write to someone in another country about your neighborhood?

Put your letter in your book.

Old and New

Does your neighborhood look just
the same as it did a year ago?

Was there something in your neighborhood
that you could not see now? What was it?

Is there something new in your neighborhood?
What is it?

What very old things have you seen this year?

Put a picture or a story in your book
about something very old or something new.

A Map of Your Own Neighborhood

Now there is just one thing
left to do in your book.

Make a map of your own neighborhood.

Make your map big enough to show the streets
or roads or places you have told about in your book.

To the Teachers Who Use This Book

The teaching-learning experiences growing out of the use of *In the Neighborhood* help second-graders understand how the people in their own neighborhood live, and why they do the things they do. As basic understandings are developed, children's ability to think clearly about neighborhood problems is consistently promoted. Most important of all, however, each learning experience stresses values and behavior which show that children are becoming responsible citizens of their neighborhood.

Five different neighborhood types provide the settings for the content of this book. Children begin the study of their own neighborhood with the neighborhood most like their own. Then they go on to study the four other neighborhoods in any order, always associating the activities described with those carried on in their own neighborhood. The last section, "Your Own Neighborhood," helps children organize and summarize what they have learned about their own neighborhood.

Each of the selections and study pages highlights one or more of the basic human activities carried on by people living and working together in any neighborhood community as indicated below.

Protecting, Conserving, and Improving Health, Resources, and Property: Lost in the Country (8-15); A Fire in the Neighborhood (80-85); After the Fire (86); Firemen Protect Us (87); Policemen Protect Us (88).

Producing, Distributing, and Consuming Food, Clothing, Shelter, and Other Consumer Goods and Services: Work on the Farm (16-18); Help for Mr. Long (26-30); Many Things Are Raised (31); Blue Jeans for Mike (89-94); Many Things Are Made (95-96); At the Store (106-113); Neighborhood Stores (114-115); People Who Work in the Neighborhood (116); Building a New Neighborhood (152-155).

Creating and Producing Tools and Techniques: Work on the Farm (16-18); Old and New Schools (32-37); Old Ways and New Ways (38); The Church Social (63-67); Old and New (122-123); Building a New Neighborhood (152-155).

Transporting People and Goods: Mail in the Neighborhood (133-135); Moving Day (146-151); Moving Things from Place to Place (162); Ways to Ride from Place to Place (163).

Communicating Data, Ideas, and Feelings: Picture Maps (39, 69, 103, 143, 180); The Newspaper Helps Judy (42-47); How a Telephone Helps Us (48); How a Newspaper Helps Us (49); Birthday Letters for Tom (124-132); Mail in the Neighborhood (133-135); Looking and Listening (142); New Friends (156-160).

Providing Education: Old and New Schools (32-37); Neighborhood House (97-102); Old and New (122-123); New Friends (156-160).

Providing Recreation: Halloween Pictures (50-54); Fun in Your Neighborhood (55); The Church Social (63-67); Neighborhood Fun (72-77); Places to Play (78-79); Doll Day at the Library (117-121); Good Times

in Your Park (141); Neighbors Play Together (170).

Organizing and Governing: Open Gates (19-
24); Rules in a Country Neighborhood (25);
Jack Learns about Rules (56-60); Neighborhood Bicycle Rules (61); Other Rules (62).

*Expressing Spiritual and Aesthetic Im-
pulses:* The Church Social (63-67); Places to
Worship (68); Neighborhood House (97-
102); The Neighborhood Sing (136-140);
Looking and Listening (142); Christmas in
the New Neighborhood (171-177).

Social Understandings Developed

David Hall's Neighborhood

Pages 8-15: In all neighborhoods there is
work to be done by members of the family.
There are big cornfields on many farms.
In farm neighborhoods the neighbors join
in the search for a lost child.
*In our neighborhood people are concerned
about lost persons and have different ways
to search for them.*

Pages 16-18: Work of various kinds is carried on in farm neighborhoods as it is in
any neighborhood.
The steps in raising corn are plowing,
harrowing, planting, cultivating, and harvesting.
*Many different kinds and sizes of machines
are used by the people in our neighborhood.*

Pages 19-25: Animals escaping through an
open gate can wander some distance and
cause damage to a neighbor's property.
A responsible farmer makes every effort to
see that his animals do not get loose.
Every neighborhood must have rules which

people in the neighborhood must observe.
The rules needed in one neighborhood may
be different from those needed in another
neighborhood.
*In our neighborhood we have rules that
will help us, and which must be observed.*

Pages 26-31: A corn picker is a large machine used in harvesting corn. A corn picker enables a farmer to pick his corn much
faster than if he were to do it by hand.
Different crops and animals are raised in
different neighborhoods.
Farm crops must be harvested on schedule.
When a farmer is unable to work, neighbors often come to help with the harvesting.
Many kinds of food are produced by people
living in farm neighborhoods.
*In our neighborhood, neighbors often help
others who are in trouble.*
*In our neighborhood people raise the things
that can be grown there.*

Pages 32-38: One-room country schools at-
tended by only a few children are often
closed.
Farm children then go to a consolidated
school or go to school in the nearest town.
Farmers often buy unused country school-
houses for their farm to house animals or
machinery.
Some schools are very old. A child's parents
or grandparents may have gone to the same
school.
Often people may think they will not like
new things or a new way of doing something, but usually they find that they like
the new way better than the old.
*Our school and other things in our neigh-
borhood may change in different ways. We
should try to look forward to and accept
such changes.*

Judy Taylor's Neighborhood

Pages 42-49: The telephone is an important way to send and receive messages.

The newspaper gives people many kinds of information and help.

It is important to know how to use the telephone and newspaper properly.

In our neighborhood many people are constantly at work so that we can have telephones and newspapers.

Pages 50-55: In every neighborhood there are ways for everyone to have a good time.

Storekeepers and owners of other business places often help children have fun.

In different neighborhoods children have good times in different ways.

In our neighborhood grown-ups help us have fun in different ways. We have different kinds of fun at different times of the year.

Pages 56-62: Accidents often lead to the making of rules to prevent similar accidents from happening.

Rules that affect everyone in the neighborhood are often made by a council.

In our neighborhood it is important for us to observe the rules made for our safety.

Pages 63-68: There are places to worship in most neighborhoods.

Neighbors may go to different places to worship on different days. People worship in different kinds of buildings.

In America people can worship in any way that seems right to them.

People in one church often help those belonging to another church to raise money for the church.

In our neighborhood there are (or are not) places to worship.

Mike Longway's Neighborhood

Pages 72-79: Seasons of the year influence the way people have fun.

In crowded city neighborhoods street areas are often blocked off and used as playgrounds. Some cities provide spray equipment which can be attached to fire hydrants to help children cool off on hot days.

Places for children to play are not the same in all neighborhoods.

In our neighborhood people have (or have not) provided places for us to play.

Pages 80-88: A town or city provides neighborhood fire and police protection for people and their property in different neighborhoods. The fire truck is kept in the neighborhood firehouse which is located so that the firemen can get to any part of the neighborhood quickly. Each person is responsible for seeing that fire and safety rules are observed.

The person who is left in charge of children is responsible for their safety.

In our neighborhood we have (or do not have) firemen and policemen who protect us and our property.

Pages 89-96: Many of the things we use are made in factories. Many, many people work in factories. Factories can produce a great many of the same article quickly. The work involved in making one article is divided among many people. One person does one thing, another does the next related step, another the next and the next until the article is completed.

In our neighborhood there are (or are not) different kinds of factories.

Pages 97-102: A neighborhood house helps make the neighborhood a better place in which to live. People go there to learn new things and to enjoy themselves in different ways. A neighborhood house is for everyone in the neighborhood.

In our neighborhood we have (or do not have) places where we can learn to do new things.

Linda West's Neighborhood

Pages 106-116: Most neighborhoods have stores and other places of business where work important to the people of the neighborhood is carried on. The goods and equipment in stores and other places of business are valuable. These things belong to the owner of the business and everyone should show respect for his property.
Neighborhood workers of various kinds help families in the neighborhood.

In our neighborhood we depend upon storekeepers and other workers for the things we use in our homes.

Pages 117-123: Libraries are for the use of everyone.
Books cost money and libraries have rules about borrowing and caring for them.
It is important to observe library rules.
Old things are interesting and often beautiful and valuable.
People are constantly developing new things to take the place of those we have now.

In our neighborhood we have (or do not have) a library.

Pages 124-135: Every neighborhood is served by a post office. It takes many people doing different kinds of jobs to carry on the work of the post office.
Post-office workers make it possible for us to send and receive letters.

People from many neighborhoods may use the same hospital.

In our neighborhood there are many things we can do to help the postman and other post-office workers.
There is (or is not) a hospital in or near our neighborhood.

Pages 136-142: Most neighborhoods provide parks for recreation.
Neighbors can have a good time together.

In our neighborhood we can do things that show we love our country.
In our neighborhood there are many things to see and hear.

Steve Bell's New Neighborhood

Pages 146-151: When a family moves, the help of movers and a moving van is usually needed.
The workers on a moving van usually load the large pieces of furniture and take them to the new location.
Moving is a very busy time and everyone involved needs to coöperate.

Pages 152-155: Many men plan and work together to build a new neighborhood.
Many different machines are used in building a new neighborhood.
Many things must be done in building a new neighborhood that are not necessary when a new home is built in an old neighborhood.

In our neighborhood men and machines are (or are not) frequently at work to improve our neighborhood.

Pages 156-160: Everyone is new in a new neighborhood. Children feel a little shy about meeting new neighbors.

193

Children from another country who do not speak our language feel even more shy and strange.

In our neighborhood there are (or are not) people who came from another country. The people in our neighborhood do (or do not) things to make newcomers feel welcome.

Page 161: There are many similarities in all neighborhoods.

There are many ways to help a new child in our country or our neighborhood feel at home. We can learn a great deal from someone from another country.

Pages 162-163: Many different kinds of cars, trucks, trains, boats, and airplanes are used to carry goods from place to place.

People travel from place to place in different ways, too.

In our neighborhood different things are used to move goods from place to place. People go places in different ways, too.

Pages 164-169: The people in a new neighborhood need to do a great many things to make their property better.

Trees can be used to improve the property of a family.

A family can take trees from a wooded area or buy trees and plants from a nursery, and replant them on their own property.

In our neighborhood people try to make their property look better and there are ways that we can help, too.

Pages 170-179: At Christmas time people make and do beautiful things to give happiness to others. In some neighborhoods all the people work together to make their houses look beautiful. In some neighborhoods people sing Christmas carols together.

Values and Behavior Traits Emphasized

The promoting of behavior consistent with the democratic values that underlie our American way of life is an integral part of every learning experience in this program. These values are fully discussed in *Living and Learning Together in Second Grade,* the "Golden Section" of the *Guidebook* to accompany *In the Neighborhood.* Examples of the behavior stressed are given below.

David Hall's Neighborhood

Pages 19-25: Learning from mistakes and acting to rectify the damage in the best possible way; assuming responsibility for knowing and obeying neighborhood rules.

Pages 26-30: Showing concern for the misfortunes of others and doing whatever is possible to be of assistance.

Pages 32-37: Adjusting to, and growing with change; appreciating the attachment of others to the familiar and remembered past.

Page 38: Appreciating values of old ways and their contribution to the development of new ways to meet current needs.

Judy Taylor's Neighborhood

Pages 42-47: Willingness to help someone who has done something nice for us.

Pages 50-55: Trying to understand the reasons behind actions that we do not like; doing one's part to make a group project a success.

Pages 63-68: Recognizing the right of everyone to worship as he pleases; gaining satisfaction from working with others to accomplish worth-while goal.

Mike Longway's Neighborhood

Pages 72-77: Acting responsibly toward members of the family; showing appreciation for kindness; recognizing the right of each person to enjoy a neighborhood recreation; appreciating the worth of each person.

Pages 80-85: Behaving responsibly and acting maturely during an emergency.

Pages 89-94: Using ingenuity to solve a problem; expressing appreciation.

Pages 97-102: Doing one's share in a group project so that the whole group can be proud of the outcome; making the most of one's abilities without hope of a reward; developing skill in an interesting activity despite handicap; showing determination in getting a job done.

Linda West's Neighborhood

Pages 106-113: Helping parents willingly by doing jobs within one's capability.

Pages 117-123: Respecting property and possession of others; using library facilities properly.

Pages 124-132: Bringing happiness to others.

Steve Bell's New Neighborhood

Pages 156-161: Doing what one can to make a new person in a new school, neighborhood, or country feel at home; helping anyone who is shy or afraid overcome these feelings.

Pages 164-168: Working with a responsible member of a team to accomplish something for the good of everyone; looking for worthwhile assets in others.

Pages 171-177: Exhibiting concern for others less fortunate; doing one's part in a neighborhood undertaking; appreciating that the greatest happiness comes from doing something for someone else.

Thinking Abilities Promoted

Children come to understand the way people live in their neighborhood and how they carry on the basic human activities in many ways. They learn by looking and listening, by reading and talking. And they learn by thinking clearly about the things they observe, read, and hear.

The content provided in the children's book and the guidance suggested in *Living and Learning Together in Second Grade,* the "Golden Section" of the *Guidebook* to accompany *In the Neighborhood* all contribute to promoting the basic thinking abilities.

The thinking abilities involved in gaining social-studies understandings developed, and the behavior traits and values that underlie our American way of life are all stressed in this program. These thinking abilities and examples of how each functions in interpretation are indicated below.

Recognizing and reacting to emotional reactions and motives: (26-30—sensing how Mrs. Long felt when she learned of the accident, how the neighbors felt and why they wanted to help); (50-55—how Mr. Read felt and why, why he changed his mind, how the children felt toward Mr. Read); (80-85—Jim's eagerness to help Mrs. Billings, his awareness of responsibility in time of danger, the anxiety of Mrs. Billings, appreciation expressed by Mrs. Billings to the Longway family); (117-121—how Linda felt about breaking her doll, her reluctance to take old doll to library, her change in attitude); (156-160—Patty and Steve's shyness about going to see their new neighbors, Peter's fear and shyness).

Making inferences: (19-24—damage caused by calves to Hall garden and how it would be replaced); (56-62—realizing what the results of Jack's accident might have been, inferring why safety rules are necessary); (136-140—Mr. Nicoli's love of America); (156-160—reason Peter came to America).

Forming sensory images: (8-15—sound of bell Mrs. Hall rang to call members of the family); (63-67—beautiful aspects of church, sounds heard in church); (72-77—noisy sounds of children frolicking in water); (80-85—Jim's yell, fire alarm, siren of fire truck, moving of fire equipment, excited voices of neighbors); (136-140—sounds of children and adults singing together in park); (171-177—beauty of neighborhood as Christmas fairyland, carols sung in hospital).

Making associations: (32-37—David's Uncle Dick and Aunt Sally Hall with their children Tom, Susan, and Peter, Grandfather and Grandmother Hall); (42-49—Mr. Ball as owner of newspaper); (80-85—Longways and Billings as neighbors in adjacent apartment buildings, the neighborhood fire station); (122-123—associating old things with time in which they were used).

Anticipating outcomes: (19-25—the results of gates being left open); (80-85—results of fire, amount of damage); (106-113—result of Bobby's antics at store); (146-151—consequences of movers arriving before Bell family).

Perceiving relationships (sequence): (16-18—steps involved in process of raising corn); (63-67—preparation for church social); (89-94—sequence of making Mike's jeans); (133-135—process involved in getting Tom's letter to hospital); (152-155—process of laying cables, sewers, and making streets).

Perceiving relationships (time): (26-31—length of time neighbors helped with corn picking and farm chores, when children gleaned corn); (42-49—newspaper deadline); (152-155—length of time needed to make the new neighborhood ready to live in).

Perceiving relationships (place): locale of each neighborhood setting, locale of natural and man-made features in each neighborhood and in child's own neighborhood.

Perceiving relationships (part-whole): specific features of each neighborhood as related to the entire neighborhood.

Perceiving relationships (cause-effect): (32-37—reason for David's reluctance to attend larger school, his reactions and adjustment to new surroundings); (63-67—why church social was held and result); (89-94—reason for making special jeans for Mike); (117-121—reason Linda's mother gave her old doll to take to the library); (164-168—reason for obtaining trees from wooded area).

Perceiving relationships (class): (31—crops used for food and clothing); (48-49—methods of communication); (61-62—kinds of rules); (68—places to worship); (78-79—places to play); (95-96—things made in factories); (114-116—neighborhood services); (141—neighborhood parks); (162-163—methods of transportation).

Making judgments and drawing conclusions: (8-15—determining that Kathy did cause trouble, though unintentionally); (80-85—evaluating action of twins, Mrs. Longway's invitation to Mrs. Billings); (136-140—judging success of neighborhood sing); (169—judging whether new neighborhood was improved through everyone's efforts).

Generalizing: (25—how all people in a neighborhood organize to protect themselves and their property); (38—old and new tools and techniques); (48-49—communication); (61-62—neighborhood rules); (68—places to worship); (87-88—fire and police protection); (95-96—manufacturing); (133-135—mail service); (141—recreational facilities); (152-155—work involved in building a new neighborhood); (162-163—ways of transporting people and goods); 169—methods of improving neighborhood); (181-189—expressing generalizations about each of the basic human activities as related to child's own neighborhood).

Strengthening memory based on observation, association, imagery, and relationships: This is stressed throughout the book.

Summarizing and organizing for the purpose of remembering: "Your Own Neighborhood."

Map Reading

Specific suggestions for teaching children how to make, read, and understand maps of their neighborhood are provided in the "Golden Section" and throughout the *Guidebook* to accompany *In the Neighborhood.*

The ability to make, read, and understand maps is promoted as children are helped to:

1) Associate imagery with semipictorial symbolism of their own neighborhood community.
2) Associate imagery of the natural and man-made features in a neighborhood community with a picture of it.
3) Perceive place relationships in terms of relative position of known points in the neighborhood community.
4) Perceive relative distance between known points in the neighborhood.
5) Perceive relative direction in terms of north, south, east, or west of known points on a floor map of the neighborhood.
6) Understand that a picture map of a neighborhood shows the natural and man-made features as if we were looking down on them from an airplane.
7) Understand that a picture map of the neighborhood shows how these features look and where they are in relation to each other.
8) Understand that on a map symbols stand for real places and things in the neighborhood, and that colors stand for land and water.
9) Understand that the symbols on a map show where places are, but not what they look like.
10) Understand that a map is the representation of an area much larger than the surface of the actual map.
11) Understand that maps of the same neighborhood may show different things.
12) Understand that a map shows which directions places and things are from each other.
13) Understand that a map shows the relative distance places are from each other.

VOCABULARY LIST

In the Neighborhood is the third book in The Basic Social Studies Program of the Curriculum Foundation Series. Although *In the Neighborhood* is intended for use at the 2¹ and 2² reader level, it has been written at the 2¹ reader level.

In the Neighborhood contains 397 different words. Of these, 188 were used in the preceding books of The Basic Social Studies Program, *At Home* and *At School*. The remaining 209 words are new in this series. Children who have completed The New Basic Reading Program through the new *Our New Friends* (1² reader) will be familiar with the 74 starred words in the list. Words with a double star appear in the Pre-Primer or Primer level of The New Basic Reading Program. Of the remaining 135

words, 54 words appear in the new *Friends and Neighbors* (2¹ reader). All the words listed below are used five or more times in *In the Neighborhood*.

In the Neighborhood has been designed to make it possible for children to read the sections in any order without encountering more than three new words per page. When there are three words on any page, one of the words is a Pre-Primer or Primer word. The vocabulary for each neighborhood section is listed below.

The following forms of known words are not counted as new and therefore are not listed: inflectional variants formed by adding *s*, *ed*, and *ing*, possessive forms, and true compounds made up of two words familiar to the children.

1 neighborhood	13 corn*	24 left	37 bus
2 buildings	very*	from*	best
farm**	three**	25 dog**	38 years
apartment	14 last*	people	39 map
3 no**	let*	walk*	
neighbors	laughed*	26 hurt	
live	15 happens	picker	
4	yard*	27 women	
5	16 garden	men	**Judy Taylor's**
	pick	28 took*	**Neighborhood**
	animals**	cribs	
David Hall's	17 use	29 noon	40 .....
Neighborhood	machines	dinner*	41 Judy
	18 raise	30 Saturday	Taylor
6	each	eat**	white**
7 his*	19 open*	Judy	42 newspaper
8 field	gates	31 food*	teaching
their	20 calves	clothes	Pretty**
9 hide	lot	32 Uncle	43 after*
sleep*	must**	Aunt	called*
10 barn**	21 mailman	33 these	please**
called*	run**	first*	44 morning*
rang	by	ago	from*
11 telephone	22 truck	34 same	45 his*
car**	met*	fall	happens
right	23 after*	35 buy*	46 telephone
12 again*	guess**	36 door*	rang
up**	got	painted*	am**
roads*			

47 hear
   must**
   if
48 hurt
   stores*
   eat**
49 year
   ago
50 Halloween
   friend**
   windows
51 Main
   Street*
   up**
52 paint*
   side
53 Saturday
   walked*
   laugh*
54 night*
   told
55 fall
   show
56 bicycle
   should
57 stop**
   jumped*
   right
58 sorry
   be*
59 council
   meeting
60 last
   safe
61 why*
   forgot
62 by
   keep
63 social
   buy*
64 busy*
   cakes
65 more
   pay
66 use
   can't*
67 hope
68 places
   worship
69 map

Mike Longway's Neighborhood

70 . . . . .
71 Mike
   city
72 hot
   street*
   run**
73 men
   car**
   jump*
74 water
   called*
   up**
75 Gramps
   am**
   started
76 after*
   laughed*
   puff**
77 Bill*
   guess**
   told
78 places
   show
79 kinds
   as*
80 store*
   four**
   heard
81 right
   fast**
   got
82 rang
   their
83 police
   stay
84 safe
   Mom
85 took*
   side
86 last*
   from*
87 protect
   keep
88 each
   should
   man*

89 jeans
   factory
90 night*
   sure
   morning*
91 don't*
   small
92 dinner*
   pretty**
   be*
93 enough
   women
94 say**
   let's*
   try*
95 food*
   eat**
   chair
96 people
   airplane
   toy**
97 baskets*
   paint*
98 Saturday
   game
99 his*
   noon
100 first*
    very*
101 best
102 prize
    thought*
103 map
    by

Linda West's Neighborhood

104 . . . . .
105 Linda
    West
106 store*
    please**
    called*
107 am**
    Bobby*
    dinner*
108 cart
    stop**
    milk*

109 must**
    bread
    hear
110 meat
    man*
111 took*
    pay
112 be*
    happened
113 Carol
    door*
    laughed*
114 places
    buy*
115 clothes
    why*
116 people
    their
117 doll**
    library
    Saturday
118 hurt
    right
119 can't*
    friends**
    thought*
120 hoped
    heard
    say**
121 today
    glad*
122 after*
    seen
123 must**
    last*
    best
124 letters
    guess**
    up**
125 hospital
    fell*
126 his*
    fast**
    got
127 post office
    morning*
128 began*
    sorry

129 sing
   ready
130 stamps
   window
131 sleep*
   doctor
132 him*
   enough
133 mail
   men
134 these
   show
135 as*
   each
136 Nicoli
   America
137 God
   Bless
138 park
   night*
139 sang*
   women
140 again*
141 .....
142 listening
   sounds
143 map
   by

Steve Bell's New Neighborhood

144 .....
145 Steve
   moving

146 busy*
   men
   dog**
147 last*
   van
   car**
148 stop**
   forgot
   Smokey
149 first*
   happen
   must**
150 run**
   if
   stay
151 right
   told
   laughed*
152 used
   machines
153 before
   ready
154 streets*
   trucks
155 yards*
   each
156 friends**
   door*
   hope
157 say**
   why*
   don't
158 hear
   him*
   am**

159 be*
   can't*
160 started
   please**
161 pretty**
   America
   from*
162 place
   show
163 people
   bus
164 together
   trees*
   four**
165 their
   teaching
166 three**
   Uncle
   Aunt
167 trying*
   took*
168 these
   guess**
   listen
169 .....
170 games
   clothes
171 Christmas
   meeting
172 fairyland
   by
   let's*
173 lights
   hide

174 night*
   hospital
175 sing
   carols
176 met*
   open*
   eat**
177 sang*
   best
178 shopping
   center
179 year
   or*
180 map

Your Own Neighborhood

181 own
   winter
182 spring
   summer
183 most
184 often
185 plants
186 .....
187 .....
188 flag
189 .....